FORTUNES FOR ALL

by

VASH YOUNG

Edited by David Harrison

Fortunes for All

by

Vash Young

Edited by David Harrison

Published by Dandi Books
115 Ruxley Lane
Epsom, Surrey KT19 9EX
United Kingdom

Printed and bound in England

ISBN 978 1 906411 00 8

Contents

Foreword by the Editor

Before I read Vash Young's book, I was a confirmed sceptic and believed that financial success for most depended more on good fortune or unscrupulousness than on ability or effort.

Vash Young and 'Fortunes for All' changed all that.

Perhaps good fortune does play a part, though, because it was purely through fortune that a copy of the original edition from 1959 was passed on to me, at a time when all my ventures seemed to be going wrong.

I soon realised – about halfway through Chapter 1 – this was a book written from the heart, by a man who had truly travelled the road he wrote about. A man who felt a deep obligation to help others find peace and fortune by sharing the lessons he learned. An ordinary man, like you and me, but perhaps with fewer advantages than most, who became extraordinary simply by changing his approach to his daily life.

Napoleon Hill could only tell us how others succeeded. Modern 'success' gurus like Oprah Winfrey and Anthony Robbins are undoubtedly successful themselves, but do they offer a model we can *copy*? For most of us they do not. The world has only so much room for TV chat-show hosts, lecturers and best-selling authors, and some of us must follow other careers.

Vash Young did write books, and did lecture, but they were not his career. He made his fortune as a humble salesman, selling life assurance to the man in the street. The difference between him and his fellow salesmen – and the reason for his astounding success – did not lie in foot-in-the-door, high pressure sales tactics, but simply in his determination to be the best he could be for everyone he met.

Reading this book and applying its lessons has certainly changed my life: I am now happier about myself, happier with my wife and family, more positive about my career and more confident about the future then I have been for many years.

Read Vash Young's story for yourself, and take it to heart: It will make a difference in your life too.

David Harrison

Epsom, June 2007

Be Kind to Yourself

MANY TIMES we read something in a newspaper, magazine or book that will stimulate us to a new line of thinking about a subject. We may have given some thought to this particular subject before, but the facts we see in print may be so astounding as to give us a new perspective. I experienced a reaction of this sort when I read in the 1958 holiday issue of Life an article devoted to American entertainment. I was astonished to read that entertainment is a $4-billion business in our country.

Although the United States in the twentieth century is responsible for many innovations in man's life, it is not the creator of his desires for fun. The article traced man's yearning for entertainment back beyond the Roman games and Greek drama, 8,000 years ago when the flute first came into being. What we can claim credit for, though, is the building of entertainment into a tremendous business, one of the giants in our national economy. Never before have so many people passed so many hours just being entertained as at the present time in our country.

The movies, radio, TV, marine shows, ice shows, the circus, amusement parks, the theatre, opera — all of these amusement outlets are devoted to the job of making fun for people. The figures given for the attendance at these events are almost unbelievable. I believe it was estimated chorus lines alone drew more than 1.5 million customers during the year. Moreover, the salaries paid to the top male and female stars and the directors, playwrights, producers and choreographers are equally impressive because they run up into the millions of dollars.

After reading the article, I started thinking about the effects of this gigantic entertainment effort. Apart from the all-important diversion factor, what is the net result after all the curtains are rung down? One conclusion easily reached was that the job of amusement for the public was by no means fun for the busy entertainers. It is a well-known fact that producers, directors, playwrights and the star performers themselves are often made virtual wrecks by the excessive strain of their jobs. To many of these people, fun-making is a very gruelling task.

What about the people who spend millions in support of the shows of their choice? Are their domestic, business, financial and social problems harmoniously solved by the amusement effort put forth on their behalf? Unfortunately the answer is *No*. Millions are left to wrestle with their same old troubles. Hospitals and mental institutions are crowded. Doctors, psychologists, psychiatrists and psychoanalysts are working overtime. People spend millions of dollars on drinking, smoking, drugs, vitamin tablets, sleeping pills, shots, tranquillizers — all in a frenzied effort to escape the self-torture of their daily routine.

At this point, every reader of this book would be justified in saying: "So what? Now that you have unveiled a world-wide dilemma, what are you going to do about it? Are you going to stick your neck out and claim you have the answer to this great problem?"

Vash Young

Well, I am going to risk saying that you would not put me on the run with such questions. As a matter of fact, I am going to surprise and perhaps annoy you by claiming I do have a good answer to this international perplexity. The answer is contained in this book. I know I have a good key to happiness because I have personally used it with almost unbelievable results.

A powerful suggestion for a more enjoyable life will be found in a later chapter. Meanwhile, you may be interested in trying out this easy-sounding happiness formula, namely, **Be Kind to Yourself.** On the surface, this is such a simple proposition, it would seem that everyone should be doing it without a reminder. Sadly enough, such is not the case. Most people are unkind to themselves without being aware of what they are doing.

I will try to clarify my point in this manner. In the Bible, we are admonished to "Love your neighbour as yourself".

I contend we generally love our neighbours far more than we do ourselves because I know very well we would not inflict on our neighbours the handicapping conduct we frequently impose on ourselves.

For instance, let us assume you have a neighbour who is in trouble. Things are not going well at home. He is having financial difficulties, is worried about his job, and in desperation he comes to you for some advice. Let's say that after careful consideration of his case you go to your neighbours with a program somewhat as follows:

8

Get up in the morning and start thinking about yourself right away.

Let the same old troubled thoughts race through your mind unchallenged.

Blow your top if things don't go just right at home.

Let highway and other travelling conditions get your goat.

Enter your office with a grouch instead of a smile.

Spend more than you earn.

Be quick to criticize and slow to praise.

Get easily upset and annoyed.

Put off until tomorrow things that should be done today.

Let yourself get out of condition mentally and physically.

Stew and fret over business and financial matters.

Finally, take a fed-up attitude toward life and fill yourself with discontent, moodiness, fear, worry and strain.

While such a program may seem a bit far-fetched, I have known many people not too far removed from it. However, the point I wish to make is that we would not think of recommending such a course to a neighbour in trouble. Then why saddle ourselves with anything of the kind?

Here is a much better plan, not only for a troubled neighbour but for one's self as well. This is a Be Kind to Yourself proposition, which anyone can use to great advantage. Simply get up each morning and firmly declare:

I Will:

Be my own best friend instead of my own worst enemy today.
Refuse to let troubled thoughts race through my mind today.
Let my family know that I love them today.
Go forth to give and not to get today.
Be careful and courteous on the highways today.
Remain poised if things go wrong today.
Make my firm glad they have me on the payroll today.
Be quick to praise and slow to condemn today.
Forget the past and have confidence in the future today.
Waste no time or money today.
Indulge in no harmful habits today.
Be not anxious or afraid today.
Finally, live today as though it were my last day on earth and try to conduct myself accordingly.

With love in our hearts, we would recommend this type of program to a distressed neighbour. With intelligent self-interest (not selfishness) in our minds, we should sell this kind of daily program to ourselves. If we want to get a good result out of life, we must forsake doing those things which produce bad results. It is as simple as that. Though it takes practice, it can be done. I know from personal experience that it can.

In the next chapter, I am going to set forth my basic reasons for writing this book. Then I am going to share with you a personal experience far more amazing to me than to anyone reading about it. After that, I will gradually lead you up to the answer which should solve most daily problems troubling you.

By Way of Introduction

BACK IN 1928 the *American* ran a story about me under the title "I Got Tired of Being a Fool". In general, the article told how the going-wrong side of life had carried me almost to the point of suicide, at which critical time a quick and tight grip on the going-right side of life pulled me out of the deep hole I was in. Hardly would I have rated a story in the American but for a Horatio Alger twist to my early start in life, for I had to win over childhood poverty and a lack of formal education.

At the time the article was published, my formula for foolish less existence was just getting under way, and I did not have too much to show for it. Chiefly I had made good progress in overcoming handicapping habits, such as drinking, smoking, self-torment, fear, worry, moodiness and the like. Freedom from these habits and emotions had helped me in my new field of life insurance, in which I gained national prominence as an agent.

What has happened since 1928 is far more amazing to me than to those who hear of my streak of good luck. For instance, I have sold $80 million of life insurance and delivered countless public lectures all over the United States and Canada. I have published five philosophic books which became best sellers.

I completed this present book at the age of seventy. If my hands were shaky, my legs wobbly, my voice faltering and my mind troubled, I most certainly would not have written this volume. However, far from being feeble, my mind is sturdy; my hands, legs and voice are steadier than ever; and my outlook on life gives me a feeling of complete dominion over current turbulent world conditions.

Actually I feel as though I am going through a second childhood, but not through a helpless stage of childhood. I am better off in all ways at my present age than at any time during my younger days. As a hard-working boy, I never knew what it was to draw a free, happy breath. Now I am at peace from the time I awaken early in the morning until I retire at the end of the day.

With Mrs. Young, I am now living in West Palm Beach, Florida; and after thirty-nine years of happy married life, I still tell her several times a day that I love her. Temporarily I have on my loafing clothes and am having a wonderful time proving it is not necessary to fall to pieces mentally or physically when reaching the best years of life.

As a matter of fact, when it comes to the subject of age, here is the way I feel about it. Having already lived many of my seventy years with what I did not know, I am entirely confident of my ability to go many more years with what I currently do know. In support of this rather optimistic outlook, I invite you to consider certain factors which seem real and very potent to me. In the first place, according to Shakespeare,

"There is nothing either good or bad, but thinking makes it so". Let's see what a bit of pardonable paraphrasing does to this idea: "A person is neither young nor old, but thinking makes him so". Thus, a person's frame of mind can largely determine whether he will carry his years gracefully.

In the United States most workers are unwanted at the age of sixty-five. They usually go off the payroll, and industry is through with them. Therefore, if a person happens to find himself alive at seventy, as I do, he would be justified in regarding himself as only five years old, because he died industry-wise at sixty-five.

Now let's make a comparison between Vash Young, age seventy according to birth records, but only five years of age according to industry; and those little shavers who are actually only five years old. Who has the best chance of survival? To my way of thinking, the odds are all in my favour. When I think of all the hazards facing the five-year-olds — the hazards which I no longer have to deal with — my path in life seems free and easy by comparison. When I was a child, we were led to expect that sooner or later we would have the measles, chicken pox, scarlet fever, mumps and similar illnesses, and we usually did. At age seventy, I no longer have to face them.

Another way of looking at age can be stated best by a quotation from the Bible:

> But they that wait upon the LORD shall renew their strength; they shall mount up with wings as eagles; they shall run, and not be weary; and they shall walk, and not faint.

In my consciousness I wait upon the Lord constantly, and I have renewed my youth. I feel better at seventy than I did as a youth in my teens more than half a century ago. I arise regularly between 5:00 and 6:00 a.m. and automatically devote a solid hour to some limbering and stretching exercises, without the least bit of fatigue.

Then after breakfast, I get in a brisk two-mile walk to and from the post office, also without fatigue. I can still catch and throw a baseball, swim the crawl stroke and ride a bike without holding onto the handlebars. I can run and not be weary, walk and not faint. But more important than all else, I can, with spiritual wings, mount up as an eagle and soar high above all the discord so rampant in the world today.

There you have in brief my main reasons for writing this new book. My past experiences have been so gratifying and my present outlook produces for me such a beautiful life that I really feel guilty in keeping my good fortune to myself.

The state of mind which saved me from self-destruction, which overcame the handicap of my lack of education, which enabled me to write five popular books, which gave me the courage to face large lecture audiences without a lesson in public speaking—this state of mind has not grown old and useless. It is more potent within me today than back in the depression years when I was changing the thinking of thousands of distressed individuals. This state of mind gives me current dominion over harmful appetites and the necessity for vitamin tablets, shots, tranquilizers and sleeping pills.

This state of mind enables me to say "scat" to such things as tension, jitters, worry, fear, frustration, chagrin, discontent, regret, doubt and all kindred attitudes. And when I say "scat," this miserable, happiness-destroying mental junk scats. I hope that by reading of my experiences and the principles I have applied to my life, you also will be able to clear from your mind any of these harmful attitudes which may be robbing you of happiness.

Vash Young

Age One to Seventy

SINCE THE FORTUNE I have to share is tied in with my own personal experiences, I have condensed a recital of my ups and downs from age one to seventy. The story is, I feel, essential to the complete effectiveness of this volume; and I have included it even though it will have a familiar ring to those who have heard it at a recent lecture or those who remember my first book, *A Fortune to Share.*

I was born in Salt Lake City on January 18, 1889. I suppose you might say I came from rather good stock. My great-grandfather was a brother of Brigham Young. I have been told that he was all man and crossed the plains five times with Mormon settlers. On Mother's side, my great-grandfather, John Sharp, was a pioneer member of the church and first president of the Deseret National Bank, the famous Mormon banking institution.

As a small boy I used to attend the Mormon Sunday school, but my participation in church activities never extended beyond my very brief Sunday school days. However, even as a youth, I learned to have great respect for the Mormon people. I was impressed by the fact that faithful Mormons did not smoke, drink, gamble or use profane language. Any religion which can free its members from such things must be a good religion. My respect for the Mormons is still very much alive within me today.

Unfortunately, my father did not seem to inherit the stable qualities of my illustrious forebears. As a matter of fact,

16

close contact with the steady citizens of Salt Lake apparently was not to his liking at all. As a result, he spent most of his time away from home and contributed very little financial support to my mother and five children, of whom I was second in line. I can remember that while I was still very young, he was off: in the Alaskan Klondike prospecting for gold. In those days, we used to wait for him to strike it rich, but he never did.

While I was still a youngster, my older brother pulled out of Salt Lake to join my father, who was then in Montana. Thus, my mother was left with four small children to bring up, and with so little help from my wandering father, we surely had a hard fight for survival. Mother frequently had to leave us children with our dear old grandma while she did housework, just to keep us in food. This situation used to fill me with youthful indignation and despair.

The first real tragedy of my life occurred when Mother simply gave up the uneven struggle and passed away when I was only twelve years old. I was completely stunned by this unexpected sad event, and for days I hid in a nearby cornfield so that no one could see my grief. We were very close, and I could not bear to think of her being gone. I felt lost without her for a long, long time.

The passing of Mother made it necessary for my sister, two younger brothers and me to make our home with our maternal grandparents. Caring for us was a burden on them because they were well along in years and had absolutely nothing in the way of worldly goods. Having reared a large family of their own, they really needed looking after as much as we did.

Vash Young

My grandfather was a carpenter by trade and a very good one. He worked at stray jobs whenever he could find them, but they always seemed few and far between. We lived in a mortgaged house upon which my father was supposed to keep up the interest payments, but he rarely did. Besides the constant fear of losing the place, we barely had enough to eat. Our menu, week in and week out, consisted of navy beans, homemade bread and oatmeal, or mush as we called it.

I had to leave grammar school to go to work while I was in the fifth grade. Being nothing but a twelve-year-old boy, I jumped at the chance to avoid school, little dreaming of the terrifying future I was letting myself in for. In my opinion, parents should insist on at least a high school education for their children. Anything less is a tragic mistake and even more so today than ever.

My first job was peddling fruit from an old dealer's wagon at twenty-five cents a day. I can remember how manly and important I felt when I turned over to my grandmother the first $1.50 I earned. The fact that I could keep none of it for myself did not bother me in the least. I even felt sorry for those kids in school who were still stuck with their studies, while I was free to peddle fruit and earn the large sum of $1.50 for so doing. How painfully ignorant I was of what was really going on — ignorant of the handicap which was being placed on my young shoulders.

My next job was labelling bottles in a soft drink factory. All day long I sat with a wet gunnysack over one knee, pasting slimy labels on soda pop and root beer bottles. Not only was I in danger of being badly cut by the frequent explosions which took place, but also the quart bottles were wired with cork stoppers. As a consequence, my hands were gashed by the constant jabbing they received from loose wires. Incidentally, my pay for this torturing job was $2.00 a week.

As the need for my meagre earnings persisted, all thoughts of any further schooling faded from my mind. What a spot for a youngster to be in! I was without the influence of either a mother or a father. I was completely missing out on regular schooling, and also I made the mistake of giving up Sunday school before learning anything about the spiritual side of life. Added to this, I was getting very little in the way of cultural training. I was simply banging away each day at some very mean tasks, asking nothing in return for what I was doing.

I jumped from $2.00 to $2.50 per week when next I landed a job in a made-to-order tailor shop. I had to clean the sidewalk, wash windows, mop floors, sew on buttons, press suits and then deliver them. Once I got an apple for a tip, but never a nickel or a dime. One day, with a suit over my arm, I ran into my former schoolteacher. When I told her what I was doing, she put her arms around me and shed a few tears.

Next I tackled the hardest job of my entire existence. It was in an inexpensive department store where I was jack of all trades. I swept the sidewalks during the summer and shovelled off snow during the winter months. Also, I had to keep a large coal-burning furnace from going out. It was up to me to keep the main floor and a large basement clean. I washed and dressed windows, replenished stock and were at the beck and call of all the clerks. I even waited on trade, and riding a bicycle I delivered heavy packages all over town. My pay was $3.00 a week.

My final job in Salt Lake City was with a florist. Once again for me it was cleaning the sidewalk, washing windows and mopping floors. In addition, I clipped the ends from flowers, changed the water, ran to the greenhouse for fresh supplies, made up bouquets and finally got pretty good at making up funeral wreaths. The last wreath I made was for my grandmother. Like Mother, she just couldn't take it any longer and quietly passed away while I was on my highest paying job — $4.00 a week.

Grandmother's death was to break up our little family group, and it was to end for me my days of childhood drudgery. A heavy sense of things hung over me during my youthful days in Salt Lake. I had been very close to the burdens placed on both my mother and grandmother. Even at Christmastime I was full of gloom because I knew it would be a dismal affair in our home. An apple, orange and some nuts in our stockings were about all we ever had. While I did not mind for myself, it did pain me to think of my sister and brothers having so little at Christmas-time.

I cannot recall having seen a bathroom until after I left Salt Lake. Our toilet facilities consisted of an outside shanty, which was very cold and draughty in the wintertime. We had no plumbing and no heat except from the kitchen stove, and we became chilled clear through whenever we got very far away from it. Of course there were no electric lights. We used coal oil lamps, the chimneys of which were usually black and smudgy. Saturday was bath night, with a tin tub placed in the middle of the kitchen floor. We took turns being the first one to bathe.

After the death of my grandmother, my sister went to live with an aunt, and the brother next to me went to live with an uncle. At this point, my father's mother managed to get enough money together to ship my youngest brother and me off to Chicago. Dad promised to repay her, but running true to form, he never did. Incidentally, my father and oldest brother were living in Chicago at this time. Had I realized how poorly equipped I was for the future, I probably would have stayed right in Salt Lake. However, I was young, hopeful and blissfully ignorant of the alarming extent of my own ignorance. I was sixteen years of age when I left Salt Lake.

I shall never forget my first contact with Chicago. We arrived in the morning, after three days and three sitting-up nights on the train. After breakfast, which I noticed Dad had allowed my brother to pay for, we were taken to a platform to await an elevated train for transportation to Chicago's south side, where my brother lived in a boarding-house.

As I looked down on the street and beheld the morning throngs hurrying to business, my heart seemed to stop beating momentarily. I had never seen so many people in my life, and the effect was a bit frightening. I suddenly felt very small, homesick, bewildered and completely lost. I felt as though I would surely get crushed when it came my turn to mingle with that mob.

Vash Young

My brother quickly got me a job in a newspaper office at the fabulous salary of $8.00 a week. To me this seemed like a fortune until I ran up against Chicago living expenses. Then it dwindled to nothing. Incidentally, Dad met me at the end of the second week, and before I knew what was happening, he had my week's salary and the new suitcase I had brought from Salt Lake. I never again saw the suitcase or the money, and even my father disappeared for about fifteen years. He left that very day for Panama without saying a word to me about the trip. Later on, I forgave all this and much more and took care of him until he died at the age of eighty-six.

My job in the auditing department of the newspaper did not last very long. With so little schooling I was not up to dealing with the calculations involved in my work. I was stumped by simple addition, to say nothing of what happened when I got to figuring the correctness of the bills I had to check. In desperation, I arranged for an attractive grade-school teacher to give me some coaching lessons at night. However, I was so overpowered by her good looks that I could not keep my mind on her arithmetic lessons, and nothing useful came of the experiment. I came to the painful realization that I had practically no equipment for survival in this environment. In Salt Lake, where my jobs called only for manual labour, I had been all right. Now however, I was suddenly called on to use abilities, thinking power and knowledge which I did not possess. I was almost frantic with despair.

To save myself the disgrace of being fired from my position on the newspaper, I went to my brother and begged him to find me another job. Since I had done fairly well during my brief experience as a fruit pedlar, I suggested he try to get me a selling job. Even at that time, intuition told me I would never succeed in any kind of office work.

Being in the advertising business, my brother managed to secure me a position with a man who represented a list of newspapers and one religious publication called World Wide Missions. I almost lost this job on the very first call. I was so petrified with fear when I stood before the advertising manager of the concern from whom I hoped to obtain an advertisement; I actually forgot the name of the publication I was supposed to be representing.

Fortunately, my new employer and my brother were good friends. Probably for this reason he overlooked the many blunders I made during my early days on the job. My salary was now $12.00 a week, which seemed quite magnificent until I began spending more than I earned. For the first time in my life I acquired a few decent clothes. However, they were all purchased on the instalment plan and had lost their glamour long before I got them paid for.

I now began meeting acquaintances of my brother. They were several years my senior, and their sophisticated ways quite dazzled me. Way down deep I knew that in this crowd I was entirely outclassed in learning and know-how. I felt uncomfortable and on the defensive most of the time. As a result, I developed a bad inferiority complex which made life miserable for me. My periods of despondency and self-torment were very painful.

In an effort to cover up my shortcomings and thaw myself out, I was lured into making the first major mistake of my life. I began drinking for moral support. At first the liquor made me deathly ill. However, I persisted in this ruinous habit, and it was not too long until I could hold my own at drinking parties. I can still recall the front I put on with absolutely nothing inside to support it except a few drinks. To complicate the situation, my brother moved to Indianapolis and took with him our youngest brother. I was left alone in Chicago in my early twenties, lacking the one thing I needed most—a spiritual balance wheel. I simply could not get hold of myself. Like a trapped animal, I paced restlessly about in my cage day and night. I was so full of fear and despair that I could not work properly. As a consequence, my job changes were frequent. To add to my difficulties, I became an almost complete wreck physically. When the draft came along in the First World War, I was rejected for any kind of military duty, and my sagging morale thereby suffered another injury. In a frantic effort to make a fresh start, I left Chicago and embarked on a road job as an advertising salesman. However, the going was difficult, and I soon began to suffer from the strain. My travelling allowance was so small that I had to put up with cheap rooms in second-rate hotels. I could eat only in beaneries, with no one but strangers to talk to. I was very lonely and actually terrified over the predicament I was in. Many times I seriously considered throwing in my hand.

Finally I gravitated to New York and landed a job with a magazine as a salesman of advertising space. By now I was in my early thirties, and while I had managed to improve my status a bit, I was still going about in a fog. I had no confidence in myself or my future. Inside, I was as mixed up as a combination salad. I spent most of my time vainly regretting the past and doubting the future. Gladly would I have accepted complete oblivion, had I known how to bring it about.

So much for the going-wrong side of life. I think you will agree that I made quite a success of it. After experiencing most of the tortures begotten by foolish, misguided living, I missed a perfect performance only by not committing suicide. The wrong way of life never had a more devoted slave than I. At the snap of a finger, I was off to do the bidding of the evil influence which has been hoodwinking human beings for centuries. If medals for stupidity had been in vogue, I surely would have deserved one.

I would now like to present my credentials on the going-right side of life. You may be justified in paying extra attention to what you are about to read because I not only lifted myself out of the deep hole I was in, but during the past thirty-seven years or so, I have lived almost a fairy-tale existence. I feel safe in promising that if you will take hold of the simple formula I began using at that gloomy time and have been using ever since, it will prove of direct help to you in dealing with some of your own current problems.

Here is what happened. While feeling extremely sorry for myself at that critical period, this thought-provoking line of reasoning suddenly popped into my mind: "What is it you want out of life — what is it you are waiting for? If you had never made any mistakes, were in perfect health and adequately educated; if you had a fine job of your own choosing, plenty of money, a national reputation and

25

everything else your heart desired — then what? Just what effect do you think an ideal set-up of this kind would have on you?"

I reasoned that under these conditions everything would be perfect. With nothing to ask for or complain about, I could quit moaning about my past mistakes and lost opportunities. I could let go of all my fears, worries and inhibitions. I could be cheerful, kind and co-operative, instead of being an old grouch. When out in the business world, I could afford to see how much I might contribute or give, instead of scurrying about to see how much I could get.

At that instant, and just as though someone had given me a swift kick, this admonition came to me: "You poor simpleton! Instead of waiting for the ideal conditions under which you believe you would be happy and content, why don't you start right now being the sort of person you think you would be if you had everything your own way?"

Believe it or not, my outlook on life changed right then and there. Something clicked inside, and in a flash I found myself intensely interested and entirely sold on this fundamental proposition : "How can I be more" instead of "How can I have more". While that may not sound very exciting to you, it was full of inspirational dynamite for me. In fact, the possibilities involved almost took my breath away. I could hardly wait to start putting the idea into practice.

I suddenly realized that here was the something for which I had been blindly searching. Here was a plan for living at which even I could be an outstanding success. While cheerfully conceding that others could have more in the way of money, jobs, housing, clothes, social position and the like, it greatly encouraged me to discover that no one on earth could be any more than I on the genuine side of life, (no one could be any more unselfish, sincere, courageous, honest, cooperative, kind and just than I.)

I reviewed the past and saw very clearly what had been wrong. Lacking most of the things I wanted very badly and without the chance of ever getting them, I had turned sour toward life. I had become a grumbler and a complainer. I was filled to the brim with fretfulness and self-pity. Instead of letting work well done produce its own unerring results, I had foolishly tried to cover up and alibi work very shabbily done. Everything I had attempted since leaving Salt Lake had been gone about in the wrong way. But now I decided that, insofar as possible, everything I attempted I would undertake in the right way.

While all thoughts of suicide had evaporated from my mind, there was nevertheless a death, because under this brand of reasoning, my former selfhood just naturally gave up and died.

Let's take a look at what died within the old Vash Young:

A demoralizing inferiority complex
A sickening feeling of being trapped by life
Despair over my lack of education
The drinking and smoking habits
Secret doubts and fears
Moodiness — self-torment — frustration
Getting easily upset and annoyed
Envying the other fellow's success
Anxiety—worries—discontent
Fretting and stewing about a job
Wasting time and money
General hopelessness with regard to the future

How did I get rid of all that happiness-destroying junk? I will try to give you the complete answer in a later chapter. At this point, I will confine myself to one line of reasoning which was of tremendous help to me. In the first place, I concluded that I was not the individual creator of such thoughts, emotions and habits and that God would never inflict on His offspring any such way of life. Therefore, I decided that this trash was an insult to God, and I resolved that these insults would no longer be hurled at the Creator through Vash Young. I let them all die within me for lack of a witness.

The Saviour said, "Except a man be born again, he cannot see the kingdom of God". A rebirth is exactly what happened to me.

28

Out of the ashes of the death just referred to, a new personality was born, made up of the following ingredients:

Self-forgetfulness
Freedom from drinking and smoking
Health and wisdom—not sickness and ignorance
A feeling of joy and independence
Gratitude—reverence—humility
Rejoicing in the other fellow's success
*The **giving** habit instead of the **getting** habit*
Poise — patience — love
Sensible living and working habits
The will to succeed

To my amazement I discovered that such an outlook on life, consisting of enduring traits of character which had made men and women outstanding and successful down through the ages, was free even to a person like me. Therefore, I took my fill of these strong spiritual qualities, and for the first time in my entire life I became happy, exuberantly happy, if you please, with absolutely none of the trappings on which happiness are supposed to depend. This is one of the strongest points I can make with you.

But becoming happy was not all that happened to me. In the first place, at this stage of my career, I met and married the lady who is now Mrs. Vash Young. She had a lovely daughter to go along with her, and suddenly I found myself possessed of a wonderful family. Then, with an apology to God for having turned my back on Him for so long, I took with me into the business world my new outlook on life, and it made me successful beyond my wildest dreams.

Vash Young

I entered the life insurance business as an agent for the Equitable Life of New York. Instead of feverishly chasing about to see how much insurance I could sell, I calmly went forth to put into daily circulation the qualities referred to in my new birth structure. I determined that I was going to get my happiness out of what I could *be* instead of out of what I could *have.* In so doing, I produced in thirty-seven years about $80 million of ordinary and group life insurance.

The simple methods I used and the volume of business I produced began to attract attention, and I started receiving invitations to address insurance meetings in and around New York. Without ever taking a lesson in public speaking, I accepted the invitations as they were presented to me. I was always glad to share with fellow agents my new outlook on life and also my simplified selling methods.

Then the *American* ran the story about me to which I have referred. A flood of congratulatory letters poured in from all parts of the country, and to my astonishment, I suddenly found myself in the limelight. So many people began coming to me for advice that I had to set aside one day a week to see them. This became known as Trouble Day in my office, and I counselled with rich man, poor man, beggar man and thief— literally so. Unemployment was running high in those days, and many cultured people were selling apples on the street corners of New York. I helped hundreds of them find jobs.

When the depression was at its height, the Life Underwriters and other civic clubs of Louisville, Kentucky, invited me to address a large, jointly sponsored luncheon meeting. The chairman explained that the entire community was badly in need of the inspirational message which he understood I was delivering. I decided to respond to this request for a lecture, and when asked for the title of my address, I suddenly felt that it should be "A Fortune to Share." This was when banks and business institutions were failing all over the country and personal fortunes were disappearing with alarming rapidity.

Right in the midst of this financial disaster I felt rich, peaceful and spiritually secure. I felt as though I really had a fortune to share with those panic-stricken individuals whose dream castles of material wealth and earthly possessions were tumbling down around their confused heads.

Therefore, I went to Louisville and faced my first large audience without a trace of nervousness. In former days, my fear would have been so great that I probably would have collapsed at the mere thought of making such a public appearance. Now, however, I was able to share my fortune of useful ideas with perfect poise, and I am grateful to relate that my message was received with standing applause by that distinguished audience.

On my return home, the Advertising Club of New York invited me to address one of its popular luncheon meetings. I responded and my talk went over the air. At the conclusion, I received a great many telephone calls, telegrams and letters from people who had listened to the address and wanted copies of it. I had the speech copied and mailed to those who requested it, but to my surprise, the address seemed to spread around like wild fire. More and more requests came in. Without waiting for permission, individuals and business organizations made copies of it and distributed them all over the country. A public-spirited man in California became so enthusiastic that he had the entire address reprinted in a newspaper. It occupied a full page, for which he gladly paid advertising rates as his contribution to the community in which he lived.

I began receiving requests for lecture engagements from Maine to California, and I filled hundreds of them. From the platform I simply told of my personal experience with both the wrong and right sides of life.

Fortunately for me, I was now brought into contact with the publishing house of Bobbs-Merrill, of Indianapolis. As a result, my first book appeared in 1931 under the title *'A Fortune to Share'*. Then followed: *'Let's Start Over Again'*, *'No Thank You'*, *'The Go-Giver'* and *'Be Kind to Yourself'*. They were all published by Bobbs-Merrill and became best sellers. They were depression books in circulation a quarter of a century ago and are now out of print.

While my ideas for these books gushed forth like water from a gurgling fountain, I had never received any training in the art of book writing, and I needed help in streamlining my thoughts. That is when two good friends of mine came to my rescue, James Derieux and Ray Giles—both capable writers. Mr. Giles helped me with *The Go-Giver,* and Mr. Derieux assisted me with the other four books. I wrote this current volume myself.

After getting the books out of my system, I settled down to two activities very much to my liking, life insurance selling and public lecturing. My insurance work enabled me to

Fortunes for All

provide needed financial protection to hundreds of families. Through lectures I shared with thousands of men and women in all parts of the country the ideas I personally had been able to use to such marked advantage.

If you knew how humble and grateful I am, you would appreciate that I have not referred to the foregoing results in order to boast or brag about my good fortune. My true motive has been to show some of the amazing possibilities behind this simple proposition of *'How can we **be** more?'*, instead of *'How can we **have** more?'* Happiness based on what we can be is within the reach of all of us right here and now.

A Chapter on Selling

I HAVE REFERRED to the success that amazed even me when I applied the principles of my rebirth to my new business of selling life insurance. I would like to describe this period in more detail so that you can see how I went about employing this philosophy and the many blessings that were mine as a result.

Out of a job, thirty-three years old, with less than $100 in my possession and with a wife and daughter to look after —that was my situation thirty-seven years ago in New York City.   I should have been greatly worried, anxious and afraid, but I wasn't because I had a new concept of life based on the fundamental proposition of being instead of *having*. I really had fun putting the idea into practical use at this critical time.

Feeling that I should stick to selling, I accepted an offer to enter the life insurance field; and on September 5, 1922, I became an agent for the Equitable Life Assurance Society of New York. Hardcastle Pennock was my manager — I shall always be grateful for his help and guidance — and at his suggestion I quickly made up a list of one hundred people I actually knew or knew of. Pennock was quite sure I could go right out and sign up most of them for a life insurance policy. I went right out, but I did not get a single signature on the dotted line. I rapidly went through that list and missed out on every prospect. I was courteously received by all those on my list, but they did not buy any insurance from me.

Right here is where I proved my dominion over fear and discouragement. I would not yield to anything of the kind. (I am grateful to report that Mrs. Young did not become discouraged either.) Rather than give way to despair, I was determined to face the problem intelligently. After exhausting my list of prospects and getting nowhere, I went off by myself and did some calm thinking. I reviewed my calls and was able to see why no one had signed up for a policy: I had not given them any sound reason for buying insurance. I had wasted their time and mine by talking generalities, such as the weather, politics, the coming world series and other trifling issues having no bearing at all on life insurance. This review of my faltering beginning enabled me to place the blame for my failure just where it belonged — squarely on my shoulders.

Then I did some constructive thinking about the business and came up with the concept that life insurance companies were simply dealers in money on a safe and convenient instalment arrangement for policy holders. I reasoned that businessmen and women really needed more money, regardless of what they might say to the contrary. Therefore, I resolved to keep myself in daily, friendly circulation and make it very easy for wage earners to acquire from me more money on a painless instalment basis. For what it may be worth, I will now reveal to you the simple plan I used.

The most important factor was my attitude toward the business. I made up my mind I was in the insurance business for keeps. I knew one of the strongest financial institutions in America was behind the contracts I had for

35

sale. Furthermore, I realized everyone was interested in money, and I began to regard my product as money. When a policy is issued and death occurs, the insurance company does not pay insurance to the deceased's family. Money is paid out, either in the form of cash or monthly income. When a loan is made, the insured does not borrow insurance. He borrows money. I saw that the whole transaction was tied in with money. Therefore, instead of waiting for the day when I could be an expert on taxation, business insurance, pension and trusts, I made my calls with wrapped-up packages of money for sale.

I dramatized the money idea with the following illustration worked out on a small filing card:

| You at Work for Dollars |
| vs. |
| Dollars at Work for YOU |
| $100 per month is 3% on $40,000 |
| $250 per month is 3% on $100,000 |
| $500 per month is 3% on $200,000 |
| $750 per month is 3% on $300,000 |
| $1000 per month is 3% on $400,000 |
| $2500 per month is 3% on $1,000,000 |

By looking at this card, an individual could tell at a glance just how much capital would be required at 3 per cent interest to equal his earned income. I was always careful to point out to a prospect that he was worth far more alive than dead and that his character, health and earning power were worth far more than he ever would be able to accumulate through life insurance or any other form of investment. While it would make a prospect feel good to realize his capital value, he could quickly see he was far short of having all of the money he needed for family protection.

Then I had a companion card showing the quarterly premium on a $1,000 policy. Instead of going after a big sale, I purposely displayed the least amount of insurance a person could buy. This may seem stupid to some, but most of my largest cases were written in this simple way. The quarterly premium was so small that it was invariably brushed aside for a much larger consideration. However, the prospect made the build-up — I didn't.

In order to get by officious receptionists and secretaries, I usually had with me a short letter addressed to the man on whom I was calling. Instead of presenting a card, I would say to a secretary, "I have a letter for Mr. Blank. Is he in?" Without asking any of the usual questions, the secretary invariably took the letter and presented it to the prospect. The letter, always written on my insurance stationery, was as follows:

> Dear Mr. Blank:
>
> Five minutes—please.
>
> Sincerely yours,
>
> *Vash Young*

I always kept handy a notebook usually filled with names taken from bulletin boards, office doors, newspapers and trade journals. I used to leave my apartment each morning with about fifteen of these letters, and they opened many doors for me.

The cards, the letters and a rate book made it easy for me to travel without a bulging briefcase to paw over during an interview. My only problem, keeping myself in circulation, was solved with my firm resolution regarding business hours: I would be in a prospect's office or on the way to one. I figured activity would be worth more to me than all the books on salesmanship I could read. This plan really paid big dividends. If I got an application, I would assume another prospect was waiting for me, and I would go straight to his office. If I didn't get an application, I still assumed another prospect was waiting for my call. I so schooled myself that when I missed a sale I was more eager for the next try than if I had succeeded. There was just no time out for discouraging idleness.

To get the feel of things, I first made some calls in the Bronx, where we lived at the time. I was encouraged when three Italian barbers in the shop where I used to get my hair cut signed up for a $1,000 policy each. Then, with the help of Mrs. Young, I wrote our vegetable man a $5,000 policy. Next, the corner paper man took a $5,000 contract with little or no urging on my part. I sold policies to several small shop owners by simply walking in off the street and showing them my cards. It seemed they all wanted to acquire some more money on my easy-instalment plan.

By now I was ready to tackle the New York City field, where I knew my prospects were endless. To put myself to a good test, I picked out a building for a cold-canvas experiment. Sauntering up to the bulletin board, I copied off five names at random and hopped into a waiting elevator. At the floor I had chosen, I fully expected to find a friendly hallway where I could look things over and get myself set for the first cold plunge. Instead, I stepped right into a large office space filled with workers who seemed to start staring at me rather suspiciously. Not having taken time to address a letter to my prospect, I became momentarily confused. Abruptly turning around, I took the next elevator to the main floor. Despite my good resolutions, I walked out of the building a bit dazed and got halfway up the block. Then a voice within me seemed to say, "Hey! If you don't go back and make those calls, you might as well quit the insurance business right now. This is the difficult side of the business you felt sure you could handle. Are you going to give up like this when there is a little unpleasantness?" That was all I needed to wake me up. I turned right around and made those calls; and while I got no business, never again was I discouraged over cold canvassing.

The tempo increased from this time on. Right and left, I presented my cards to almost everyone with whom I came in contact. This meant that I was talking about money all day long and often far into the night. I stopped an acquaintance on the street one day, but, being in a hurry, he suggested I call at his office the next morning for a further discussion of my favourite subject. When I called, he seemed surprised to see me, and during our discussion he would look at me and smile. Finally I got his application for a $10,000 policy. As I was leaving he said, "Vash, did you go to your office this morning before calling here?" When I answered in the negative, he said, "Well, when you get to your office, you will find a letter from me which should give you quite a laugh." When I read his letter a little later on, I did get a laugh because in it he told me he had changed his mind about talking things over with me and asked me not to call.

There was a carpenter doing some repair work in a place where I called one day. As I was leaving I showed him my cards and asked if he would like to acquire a little more money on an easy-payment plan. The result was that he invited me to call at his home that evening, and of course I did. I obtained his application for a $10,000 policy, and later I insured his uncle and several of his friends. While I was now picking up $5,000 and $10,000 contracts, I always presented my $1,000 illustration.

One time I got the head of an advertising agency to let me present my cards to the key members of his organization. Within a short time, I insured twelve of them in amounts ranging from $3,000 to $10,000. When I called one day to thank him for his fine co-operation, I said, "Incidentally, I owe you an apology. I have been so busy arranging more money deals for several of your fine staff members that I have entirely overlooked you." He smiled good-naturedly, went over my cards with me, and I wound up with an application for a $50,000 policy with a very high premium. All of these cases came through simple, friendly discussions of the financial problem confronting each individual. Invariably I would say, "Personally I wish with all my heart that you did not need any more life insurance. However, if you feel you do, I will be glad to help you get it on a rather painless payment plan."

One day I presented my letter to a key man in a very large corporation. To my delight I was shown right in to his impressive office. He greeted me with, "Mr. Young, I don't want to buy any more life insurance, but your courteous request for an interview entitles you to the five minutes you have asked for." I thanked him for his courtesy, quickly showed him my cards and within an amazingly short time, I had his application for a $65,000 contract. While he did not want any more life insurance, he did decide to add $65,000 to the protection of his family.

I recall the time I was summoned for jury duty lasting for a period of three weeks. I fortified myself by collecting many names of persons in the vicinity of the courthouse. Getting excused for several hours one day, I headed for an important man with whom I had talked previously. He almost floored me by saying, "Vash, I was just about to send for you. I am going to buy a substantial amount of insurance and will be glad to have you handle the deal." I got his application on the spot, arranged for the examination, ordered out a $250,000 policy with an annual premium of $8,300 and placed the business. Even on jury duty, I led the entire sales force of the Equitable for the month in paid-business volume. I recall the time I telephoned a man almost once a week for an entire year. He always had some excuse for not seeing me, but he kept on suggesting I telephone again. Finally one day he said, "Young, I can't seem to think of a darn reason why you should not come right over here if you want to." I wanted to all right, and after seeing my cards, he became interested in a retirement annuity policy with a $5,000 annual premium. Before signing the application, however, he wanted me to discuss it with his wife. I talked with her, and, to shorten the story, I wound up with a $10,000 annual premium deal. This experience reveals the importance of patience in sales work.

On one of his trips to New York several years ago, a Chicago man signed with me an application for a $100,000 single premium annuity in the Equitable. While waiting for the contract to be issued, I was instructed to obtain from another company an alternate contract so that a rate comparison could be made. Thus, I was now waiting for the issuance of two $100,000 policies, and I don't mind confessing that I felt very good over the deal. My prospect seemed genuinely interested. I knew he had the necessary premium money, and I was fully confident of my ability to place at least one of those contracts.

Then the roof suddenly caved in on me. At my home one Friday night, I received a long distance telephone call from my prospective annuitant. He explained that after thinking things over, he had decided against my plan. He apologized for having taken up so much of my time but requested rather firmly to be relieved of all further participation in the deal. In a voice entirely free from agitation, I calmly asked when he expected to be in New York again. When he told me Monday morning, I requested one more brief interview, and he agreed to see me.

Since his call had come through on a Friday night, I was faced with a very gloomy week end. Right here I put into practice my theory of being vs. having, and it worked out beautifully for me. I proved to my great satisfaction that the possible loss of the business involved was powerless to make me unhappy. I called on my fortune of right thinking to sustain me, and by the time Monday morning rolled around, I knew I was completely in control of my emotions if the deal finally fell through.

Promptly on time, I walked into my prospect's hotel room, and there we began discussing anew the entire transaction. I was at my selling best that morning and had a good answer for every objection he raised. With a smile he finally said to me, "Mr. Young, I can see you are very well sold on this annuity deal. Which contract do you recommend I take?" Without a moment's hesitation I replied, "Take them both; they may never come your way again." That's exactly what he did. I walked out of his room with cheques totalling $200,000 instead of the $100,000 I originally hoped to get. In this connection, I wish to point out I was a double winner. By refusing to collapse within myself when the deal apparently had fallen through, I proved my ability to maintain a peaceful state of mind in the face of business discouragement. Furthermore, I emerged from the encounter with double the business I had expected to receive.

These experiences illustrate the surprising success I had putting into practice the general proposition of *being* rather than *having*. I can give you an idea of a more specific application of this principle with the terms *giving* instead of *getting*. In an effort to prove that in *selling* giving is oftentimes superior to ***getting***, I will conclude this chapter with three actual experiences you may find hard to believe.

Case 1. One day an acquaintance telephoned and invited me to lunch. During the luncheon he explained that on the previous day his wife's mother had died and his wife had become prostrated with grief. Since she was in no state to appear at the funeral the next day, my friend asked me to go with him to his Long Island home after lunch and attempt to say something to his wife which would enable her to get hold of herself. Now I did not stop to consider whether I had the time for this chore or whether it would be a profitable thing for me to do. I went with the man to his home, and it did not take me long to dry his wife's tears with just a little tender reasoning. I pointed out that she was doing exactly what her mother would not want her to do and what God did not want her to do.

A few minutes after I left the house, I was later told, the wife's tears were all dried, and the funeral took place the next day. I promptly forgot about the incident, but the law which rewards the giving habit apparently did not forget the matter.

A brother of my friend's wife was a prominent New York businessman. When he heard about my experience with his sister, he expressed a desire to meet me. A luncheon was arranged; and after thanking me for what I had done, this man exclaimed, "I understand that you are in the life insurance business. I have a fourteen-year-old boy. Do you think I should have some insurance on his life?" When I replied that I did, the man asked me to let him know what I would recommend. Within a couple of days I presented him an illustration based on a $25,000 policy. To my utter amazement, the gentleman I am talking about wound up by arranging for $1 million of insurance on his fourteen-year-old boy. Throughout the negotiations, what do you think I was doing? Believe it or not, I was trying to talk him out of such a large amount of insurance on his boy. I thought he was overdoing it.

Case 2. One day during the depression a stranger called at my office in New York to seek some advice. It turned out that he was an actuary, a mild-mannered sort of person who had been frozen out of his job. With great earnestness I expounded my theory of *How can I be more* instead of *How can I have more?* I must have been rather good that day because this man left my office in a changed and also a very grateful frame of mind.

I never expected to see the man again. However, one day he again showed up at my office and explained he had come in to thank me for my kindness to him when he was out of a job. He said he now had a good actuarial position and wanted to introduce me to the officers of a company considering a large group annuity. Again it astounds me to relate, the company went ahead with my plan, and the first check I turned over to the insurance company was for $5 million.

Case 3. Several years ago I was instrumental in arranging for a president of a large New York corporation a sizable bank loan at a favourable rate of interest. When the transaction was completed, the man was so grateful that he wanted to pay me a fee. I sincerely explained there was no fee; his friendship was ample reward for what

I had done. He was not satisfied to let the matter rest there, and knowing I was in the life insurance business, he suggested a review of his policies in order to find out what effect on his estate the new loan was having. Without too much difficulty I discovered a real need for an additional $200,000 of personal insurance which he promptly agreed to take. For the third time it astounds me to relate, within a week he ordered over the telephone $1 million of business insurance for his company. The premiums involved in this entire transaction totalled approximately $50,000 per year.

In the beginning I knew nothing of the possible existence of any of this business. However, I had learned a little about the power of *giving*. With a desire to give something, I did what I could for those three men. To show their appreciation, they wanted to repay me, and the amazing results speak for themselves.

Sympathy for Business Leaders

FROM THE EXPERIENCES I have related you can see that I was able to reconstruct my life and transform an unhappy life of failure into a success. What about people who are successful in business? Are their problems and worries serious enough for them to change their lives as I did mine ?

During my days of selling insurance and lecturing I have had the opportunity of meeting many people prominent in business, and I have become acquainted with many of their problems. My sympathy goes out to our business and professional leaders, the ones with the big jobs and the big responsibilities. The pressure is on them most of the time. As one heavy chore is finished, another one comes up for consideration. Hour after hour and day after day, they deal with troublesome situations. Even at lunch and between golf shots they continue to talk about and ponder over the important deals in which most of them are concerned.

One day I attended a business luncheon at a well-known New York club composed of members prominent in their respective fields. They were there that day in large numbers, looking forward with interest to an address to be given by a laboratory technician recognized as an authority in his field.

The audience was not disappointed, for the speaker discoursed at some length on the impetus being given to general conditions by scientific inventions in the making. He knew his subject well, and as he told us of the mechanical wonders of the future, we were given the feeling an amazing era was just around the corner.

At the conclusion of the luncheon, I remarked to my host that two very definite impressions had been made upon me. First, the mechanical perfection so much in evidence today will be greatly increased in the future. Second, the saddening evidence of human imperfection we encounter in all directions seems to get worse instead of better. When asked for a fuller explanation of what I had in mind, I mentioned some of the spectacular feats now being performed in atomic research, aviation, radio, electronics, shipbuilding, communications and television and the achievements of scientists and engineers in many other fields, some of which are almost beyond comprehension by the man in the street.

Then I called attention to the display of human imperfection constantly before our gaze. I pointed to the fact that many, almost certainly the majority, of the splendid business and professional leaders at that luncheon were badly out of shape. It was my opinion, and one I felt qualified to express, that probably not more than one in ten of that group of perhaps 250 men would be able to pass a standard examination for life insurance. Not only did their bodies plainly reveal striking evidence of the lack of good physical condition, but their facial expressions also betrayed the great strain under which they were labouring.

Among our business and professional leaders today are some of the finest men and women on earth. Most of them are well bred, well educated and highly talented in their professions. These people hold, and deserve to hold, the most favoured positions and are paid the highest salaries. They live in good homes and are surrounded by all the comforts and advantages money can buy. They wear the finest clothes, move in smart society, are the largest buyers of government bonds and give liberal support to many charitable institutions.

As a rule they are quite unselfish even though they may seem otherwise to those who live under less favourable circumstances. In addition to their financial support of worthy causes, they are in a great many instances donating their time and energies to the communities in which they live, asking nothing in return.

As a class they are broad-minded and capable of viewing in an unbiased manner the conflicting issues constantly facing us. Many of them have no church affiliations, but they recognize and respect the rights of others to attend their own religious services or to do anything else they may choose.

These men and women seem to have everything they want or need. While they work very hard, they also play very hard. Many of them ride hobbies which seem to give them plenty of relaxation and pleasure. Some of them have country homes to which they give a great deal of attention, where they have gardens and conservatories in which they take great pride. Some go in for outdoor sports and strive to become experts in their favourite pastime, such as golf, skiing, swimming, tennis and kindred activities. Others choose hobbies requiring less physical effort, like collecting first editions, stamps or works of art.

I have a feeling, however, that despite the pride and pleasure their avocations bring them, these top-flighters are missing out on something. I feel they could be greatly benefited by casting aside some of their sophistication and getting back to the simple side of life. I should like to get them to accept, like little children, some of the ideas I am putting forth in this book, particularly the main idea, which comes a little later. Perhaps the following example will clarify the point I want to make.

I know a man for whom I have great respect and admiration. He is an admirable person, and I value his friendship very much. He graduated from college with high honours, and during his college days he played many leading roles in campus life and in fraternal activities. He was editor of his college paper and distinguished himself in many other ways.

He has made intensive studies of astronomy, natural history, chemistry, higher mathematics and science and has found an explanation satisfactory to himself concerning all mineral, vegetable and animal life. You can judge from all this that he is a well-informed person.

Fortunes for All

My friend is a prodigious worker. He holds an important executive position with a New York corporation, and he does a magnificent job. He knows what should be done, and with the help of capable assistants, whom he has carefully trained, he has the ability to get things done in a very efficient manner.

In addition to his regular job, he helps direct several other important activities directly allied with the business in which he is engaged. At the end of a hard day at his office, he can usually be seen hurrying for his train with a briefcase full of business papers which he tackles after having dinner with his family.

He and his wife are very gracious hosts, and their social life is quite active. He is a good conversationalist, can talk intelligently on almost any subject under discussion, and he can play the piano in a very pleasing manner.

Quite a person and quite a situation, wouldn't you say? He and his wife are well off financially; he is a pronounced success in business; he is widely and favourably known in business and social circles; he has some fine children, who are being very carefully reared; and, on the surface, he is a man of good fortune.

However, looking a little deeper into his situation, one can see this man is not so well off as he seems to be. In the first place, because of business strain he has developed high blood pressure, which not only endangers his life but also disqualifies him for standard life insurance. On top of this, he recently had to undergo a serious operation which kept him away from his business for about two months. While in the hospital and during his convalescent period, his enforced idleness drove him almost to the point of distraction.

Running true to form, his intellectual nature searched for and found an exhaustive explanation of his illness. In great detail and with the use of highly involved medical terms, he can tell exactly how it all happened and why. He has a very scholarly explanation for everything, right down to the most minute detail.

Because of overeating and over drinking at social functions, business luncheons and conventions, this man is overweight. Every so often he goes on a diet which is absolute torture to him. Incidentally, the benefits are not lasting because as soon as he takes off a little weight, he starts indulging in the kind of food and drink which puts it right back on.

In addition to the foregoing, he smokes incessantly. He claims he does this to quiet his nerves, but I have observed that smoking has just the opposite effect on him. He is very nervous and jumpy and is getting more so all the time. Every now and then he makes a valiant effort to quit smoking, but after a short period of abstinence he goes right back to the habit which seems to be completely wrecking his nervous system.

Now what do we see? The answer is very simple. We see a highly successful business executive who exercises intelligent control over everything but himself. He runs his business and social affairs very smoothly, but when it comes to his own state of being, he is sadly out of control. He has a scholarly, intellectual answer for all forms of life except his own life.

Now this man is not complaining. He probably realizes he is steadily playing a losing game, but he is not greatly concerned. He has lived a full and interesting life and is not afraid to die. As a matter of fact, he has admitted to me that when his time comes he will be ready to go. While he has expressed the hope of finding a better state of existence beyond the grave, this really does not make much difference to him, or so he claims.

In one respect, my friend occupies a reserved seat in the grandstand. However, almost any bleacherite is getting far more satisfaction out of the game of life. I hope you can now see why I headed this chapter, "Sympathy for Business Leaders". My friend (and there are millions like him) is in real need of help. Of course, I think I know how he can get this help; otherwise I would not have reviewed his situation in such detail.

The Capital Value of Thought

I CITED THE CASE of a successful businessman who apparently had control over many things concerning his life but lacked control over the most important thing— his own state of being. Besides the injury to his health, business and family, let's see what other factors are involved when the individual does not have complete dominion over himself.

Compare 97 cents with $500,000. A great difference, is there not? Such a comparison is intended to reveal the amazing disparity between what we see and what we do not see. For instance, we can see the human body, which has a chemical value of approximately 97 cents. But we do not see the thinking which motivates a human body. This thinking may be worth $500,000.

What produces income in the form of salary or wages? Is it the individual's bodily form? No. Deserted by thought, a bodily form does not have the intelligence or the power to produce anything. By itself, it is mindless and worthless. Then what does produce earned income? It is the thinking of the individual.

Assume, if you will, an individual earns $15,000 a year. Well, 3 per cent of $500,000 is $15,000. Therefore, it would take the huge sum of $500,000 safely invested at 3 per cent to equal an earned income of $15,000. If you dwell on this idea carefully, you will begin to place a new valuation on your own thinking.

Here is something for wives to consider. A wife not only waves good-by to her mate every morning but also temporarily separates herself from $500,000, should her husband be earning $15,000 a year. By the same calculation, even if her breadwinner is earning only $3,000 a year, a wife is waving good-by to the potential sum of $100,000. Because thought is the chief producer of money, it is highly important for a wife to send her husband on his way to business in a peaceful frame of mind. For instance, let us assume a married couple live in a house valued at $30,000. Upon awakening in the morning, they do not take sharp instruments and begin hacking away at and disfiguring the inside walls, nor do they begin pelting the house with mud and rocks just as the husband is taking off for work. They would not think of doing such outlandish damage to a home worth $30,000.

Now let us assume the husband in this imaginary situation earns $15,000 a year. Let us further assume it is a common occurrence for this couple to start the day with heated arguments which continue right up to the angry shouts hurled at each other as the wage earner starts for his place of business. In this situation, the sharp instruments of physical destruction are not to be compared to the damage done by sharp tongues, as simple arithmetic shows. Remember the house has been valued at $30,000. But what about the economic value of the income producer? On the basis of his salary of $15,000 per year his capital value is $500,000. Therefore, the physical damage which might be done to the house does not compare to the mental damage done to the income producer by stupid family squabbles.

Here is a suggestion to all wives who may be reading these lines. If an argument takes place in your home and your man leaves for work in a huff, wait until you think he has reached his place of business, get him on the telephone and say," Hey, you big dope, I love you!" Then hang up quickly without giving him a chance to say a cross word in reply. In my opinion, this simple act will do more to restore harmony than anything else which could happen after a quarrel. Remember a man needs mental harmony in order to make a continuing success of his business.

If we were half as careful of our mental property as we are of our physical well-being what a difference it would make. For example, a cut finger receives immediate care. Also, a stomach-ache or a pain in some other part of the anatomy is sufficient cause for much nursing and coddling. But when our feelings are cut or bruised by some unpleasant experience, we often aggravate the injury by keeping the wounds wide open with thoughts of anger, resentment and a smouldering sense of injustice. This is all wrong. We should take better care of our mental property because it is by far our greatest asset.

Most valuable possessions are put carefully away for safekeeping. Money, stocks, bonds, life insurance policies and other things of value are placed in banks or safety deposit boxes. But how about the greatest asset of all, our daily thinking? Is this treasure put safely away? No! It is dangerously exposed each day to the turmoil in which we are living and to the disturbing news relayed to us by radio, television and press. It is subjected to the commotion of business and social life. Thus, our greatest asset is in danger of being reduced to the value of a thin dime. How? By thoughts and emotions let into our consciousness with which we can make neither progress nor money.

Here is a sample of what I mean. A man I know earns $30,000 a year, but look at what he is doing with his most valuable possession, his daily state of mind. He does not like the way things are being run in Washington and gives vent to his feelings at every opportunity. His bitter complaints over the taxes he has to pay do not seem to lower them any. He has stubborn views on politics and religion and as a consequence gets into many heated arguments. He has three lovely children, but, instead of enjoying them as he should, he allows the youngsters to get on his nerves. He has a fine wife with whom he is constantly bickering over some trifling domestic affair. When no one is around but the members of his family, he is grouchy, and the result is a strained and extremely unpleasant home life.

This man is very intelligent in the handling of his business affairs as evidenced by the fact that he is able to earn $30,000 a year. However, his very unintelligent handling of his emotions is constantly having a damaging effect on his thinking. The running of things in Washington will not be affected by his violent complaints to his friends and business acquaintances. Taxes will not be reduced by his objections to them. But his children will be handicapped by his impatience and irritability, and his wife will get neither peace nor comfort out of his temperamental outbursts.

Besides the harm done to others, this man is literally wearing himself out over conditions he cannot control. Instead of trying to govern these uncontrollable outward conditions, he should practice the art of not allowing them to control or affect him. One reason for his tantrums is his failure to recognize the tremendous value of his mental property.

Here is another sad case of the self-inflicted damage which can be done to mental property. Many years ago I knew an individual who occupied a very prominent position in the publishing field. Accompanied by a friend one day, he went for lunch at a restaurant where he was well known and as a rule got prompt and efficient service. On this particular day, however, the restaurant was very crowded. He was seated at a table vacated by another luncheon party, and the demi-tasses and dessert dishes had not yet been removed.

A new waiter on the job had his hands full with other luncheon guests who had already placed their orders. The man I am telling you about became very annoyed over the delay in getting his accustomed service and protested to the head waiter a couple of times, but without effect. Finally he became so exasperated that he yanked the tablecloth, with all the soiled dishes, right to the floor. Of course, there was an awful clatter, and that entire dining room filled with prominent people felt the embarrassment of this public display of bad temper.

This person's salary in excess of $30,000 a year made his business thinking worth more than $1 million. However, he had so little control over his emotions that he made a jackass of himself in public. Incidentally, not long after this incident he lost his job. Talk about the destructive power of termites; lack of thought control is constantly destroying mental property of far greater value than homes and business properties.

So far I have discussed the value of business thinking, but what about office and plant politics, suspicion, envy, jealousy, greed, hate, fault-finding, dissension and a hundred and one other apparently worthless things? Can these thoughts, emotions and influences be profitably commercialized? I don't think so. One cannot transform negative and destructive things into assets. The foregoing mental junk is like a collection of bad debts; nothing can be realized from them, and they only make a bad showing on the balance sheet.

By the way, have you ever stopped to consider how such destructive influences gain entrance into business organizations? Do such thoughts enter by means of inanimate, unthinking objects, such as desks, fixtures and plant equipment? No! They can be put into action only through the minds of officers and employees. They can be nurtured and brought to full poisonous growth only through the minds of the personnel. Keeping such destructive thought forces from working through his mind should be the duty of each individual.

When you have a job, you are paid for your thinking, and it naturally should be devoted exclusively to your firm's business during working hours. Let us assume you have many things on your mind. You have made some mistakes in the past; you are in financial straits; you are having some trouble at home; you are not satisfied with your job; you are worried about the future — all of these problems and many more may be on your mind.

Inasmuch as your employer cannot see your thinking, it is very easy for you to devote much thought to your personal situation right at your desk, your machine or on the way to a prospect's office, if you are a salesman. Except for one important factor you would be perfectly safe in giving only part of your thinking to your job: business promotions and salary increases are not likely to be won with part-time thinking. Even though such thinking cannot be seen, it is reflected in the work that is done. Therefore, if an individual is not getting along as he should, it is probably because not enough of his thinking is devoted to the work he is paid for doing.

The ideal way for any individual to handle himself while on his job is to make sure he would be in line to receive a pay raise instead of a dismissal if the boss could see his thinking.

The Space Age

WITH THE GREAT achievements of scientists and inventors in providing new discoveries to make life easier for us, there is a likelihood we may be lulled into the belief that if we wait long enough. the people who do great things will eliminate all our problems and do away with the longstanding barriers to human happiness.

In the field of space travel the recent progress has been astounding, and it leads us to believe that a new kind of life is in store for many people. For instance, during the 1958 holiday season the United States startled the world by launching the largest single object ever put into orbit by man. This was the mighty Atlas 10, an object as long as a Pullman car and weighing 9,000 pounds.

An outstanding feature of this space gadget was a transmitter which accepted messages and then sent them back to earth. This mechanism enabled President Eisenhower to deliver the first message ever sent from outer space. Appropriately, it was a "Peace on earth, good will to men" greeting. During its relatively short span of life, this rocket circled the earth in orbit at more than 17,000 miles per hour.

Then on January 2, 1959, the Russians surprised the world by launching a rocket which started off with the nickname "Moonik". However, the name did not last long because this rocket was travelling so fast that it sailed right past the moon, before going into orbit around the sun. It is now called "Mechta" (meaning dream) and is orbiting at a distance of 22 million miles from the earth.

The space age is upon us for sure, and we can expect some dazzling developments. With the earth becoming more densely populated, it is conceivable that many venturesome people may want to go live in outer space. When considering all the other barriers being shattered daily, we need not be surprised at anything that takes place in our new space age.

Less than 500 years ago humans were labouring under the delusion the earth was flat. Then along came Columbus to prove the earth was round, and this discovery released the world from all sorts of physical barriers. For instance, in 1620 the Pilgrims landed at Plymouth Rock and established the first settlement in New England. That was only 339 years ago; but just think of what has happened in our country alone since that time. Today the United States is the most powerful nation on earth. This accomplishment in itself is far more impressive to me than anything which may develop in the conquest of outer space.

It is easy to remember the day in 1927 when Charles Lindbergh electrified the world by making his famous solo flight from New York to Paris. He made the trip in thirty-nine hours and was out over the Atlantic alone all night long. Today jet planes make it possible for a person to lunch in New York and on the same day have dinner in London or Paris. Ocean flying is now so common we think nothing of it, even when records are broken with monotonous regularity. Living on a space ship up near the moon is not at all far-fetched as far as I am concerned.

Fortunes for All

What happened to the unbreakable four-minute-mile myth? It has completely disappeared from the minds of the people, since Herb Elliot came along and broke it ten times in one year. Records in swimming, running, track, golf, tennis and baseball are likewise being broken constantly.

Just as breath-taking as the conquest of physical barriers is our progress in providing new comforts and conveniences. New home gadgets are bewildering in their profusion as they are presented to the public in glittering television and national advertising mediums. These inventions are designed to save us work and provide us with pleasure.

But how about John Doe, Mr Average Citizen and his family? Where does he stand in the midst of all this splendour? Has the brightness of the world in general put lustre into his life? Is he happy and gay over all the conquered barriers and also all the comforts available to those who can afford them? Unfortunately, the answer is No. John Doe is still up to his neck in trouble, just as he has been for centuries past. While the world at large continues to break through barriers on a wide scale, John Doe is still bound by the same old routine handed down to families from generation to generation.

A pattern for human behaviour seems to have been established by Adam and Eve way back in the Garden of Eden when they yielded to temptation and sacrificed a life of ease and contentment for banishment into a world of toil. Ever since that time, men, women and children have been tempted into mistake-making of one sort or another, and for these mistakes they have been punished accordingly.

Then the son of Adam and Eve named Cain had the mark of a murderer placed on him, and the baneful influence of murder has continued to motivate man down through the ages with the sad results familiar to all.

I could go on with endless examples, tending to show that human conduct today is just about the same as it always has been. Under new names, new living conditions and with new faces, we are proving that our current behaviour closely patterns the Biblical history of the human race. We are simply spinning around in that ancient orbit from the cradle to the grave.

Getting back to "Mechta" for a moment, here is something worthy of deep consideration. It is estimated this rocket may be in circulation for perhaps a million years since it will lead a completely stress less and stainless existence. It is a physical system in perfect equilibrium out where there is no force to pull it back. This idea of a body in equilibrium certainly ties in with our job of striving to break the human conduct barriers which fence in the individual on all sides. These barriers are made up largely of long-standing habits and emotions such as the following: smoking, drinking, gambling, morning grouchiness, wrangling at home, and run-ins with office associates, smarting under criticism, frustration, moodiness, self-torment, secret fears, overspending, overeating, procrastination and poor workmanship.

There you have some of the barriers — the friction, if you please — which make life so difficult for the individual spinning about in his daily orbit. As Arnot has said, "Men are born to trouble at first, and are exercised in it all their days. There is a cry at the beginning of life and a groan at the end of it." For the average individual, that is the way it is and always has been. All of the scientific advances being made are of very little use to the individual and his personal problems. He is stuck with himself, stuck with what he thinks and does, stuck with his own friction. Self-help is what he needs most of all, and that is what I am trying to supply in this book.

Try This Experiment

UP TO THIS POINT it seems I have talked only about troubles. That is, I related the difficulties I had, recounted a few cases of pressure on businessmen and pointed out that men have had personal problems as long as they have existed on earth.

Since I have stressed the need for self-help and indicated my intention to supply it in this book, you may be wondering when I am going to start. Now I am going to ask that you try an experiment. It is simple in its execution, but the results may be more powerful than you imagine. It will give you a first-hand experience in applying my proposition of being instead of having. Get off by yourself with a pad and pencil and write out your own ticket for a happy and successful life. By that I mean put down all of the things you would like to have or be. Don't tell anyone what you are doing but be perfectly honest and, above everything else, do not stint yourself in any way. Perhaps you would like to be President of the United States. All right, put that down. Or perhaps you would be satisfied just to be president of your company, in order to bring about certain changes you feel could be made to advantage.

If you are not interested in business along strictly commercial lines, perhaps you would like to enjoy the limelight by being a popular Broadway, television, radio or moving picture star. If you are a sports enthusiast, perhaps you would like to be a champion golfer, tennis player, and swimmer; or maybe you would like to be one of the all-time greats in baseball or football.

Of course, you should include perfect health on your list. It goes without saying that you would like to have plenty of money so that you would never have to be worried over financial matters. Undoubtedly there is a particular place you have always wanted to live and under the ideal conditions about which you may have been dreaming. You might want to go on a world tour with no time limit attached to it.

You may have some hobbies you would like to follow, such as painting, writing or just plain fishing and hunting. You would, of course, want to leave yourself with some worth-while objectives to work toward because having everything you wanted, with nothing to do but clap your hands to have your wishes gratified, would make life somewhat a bore. Therefore, be sure to leave yourself with something exciting to look forward to.

After compiling your list, please take a good look at it to make certain you have not overlooked anything. Be sure you have outlined for yourself a state of existence that would make you very happy if the whole program could be yours. Then try to imagine that very suddenly every wish has been gratified. Things are exactly as you would like to have them with nothing left undone. You are sitting on top of the world, so to speak. What a grand spot for you to be in!

Now heed carefully this next suggestion. It could be one of the most important ever made to you. After imagining every wish has been granted, then go one step further. Start in being the ideal person you think you would be if you had everything your own way. Remember you have written out your own happiness program; every wish has been granted you. Therefore, you have nothing to complain about and no reason to be grumpy about anything. The world is yours, and you can well afford to be one of the noblest persons alive. Just be that person.

Does the foregoing suggestion seem like a trick, a form of self-deception? Does it sound like a silly childlike game? Well, I will admit it is a game, but it is the greatest game you can possibly play. It is the game of being vs. having.

What if you went about your daily affairs in the frame of mind appropriate to one whose life was worked out to his entire satisfaction? You would be a remarkable person, would you not? But, you may say, things are far from being worked out in accordance with my wishes. Life is a torment; therefore, how can I go about in a contented frame of mind? To me, the world is a sour proposition, and I cannot help feeling bitter about it.

Such implied reasoning on your part enables me to stress a very important point. You cannot sweeten a sour situation with more sourness. It takes sweetness to do the trick. That is why I urge you to go about your affairs as though you were sitting on top of the world. Be the real, joyful thing despite unpleasant conditions. In this way, you prove your domination over discontent and unhappiness. As you persistently and consistently live your ideal, your position is bound to improve.

People all over the world set for themselves desirable objectives and live continually in a state of self-torment when they do not attain them. Their thoughts and efforts are so bent on the objectives that they often forget it may be necessary to make certain fundamental changes within themselves to reach the goal they have set. It is difficult to run uphill with downhill thoughts, emotions and habits. Your thoughts should be appropriate for the direction in which you want to go. Start at being a good person, and good things will be added unto you.

For instance, I met a friend one day; and after visiting for a few moments, she exclaimed, "Oh! I do hope the weather will be nice on Sunday, because we have a new car, and I shall be heartbroken if we cannot take the trip we have planned. Therefore, I have been praying for sunshine over the week end."

I replied, "Well, for your sake I hope the sun does shine, but let me tell you of a much better prayer to make. Why don't you pray for the ability to have a good time over the week end regardless of weather conditions. Then you will be sitting pretty no matter which way the weather turns."

Please go over your list again. If your every wish were gratified and you did not turn into a person of exceptional character, what good would it all do you? If you had everything you wanted and still were discontented, what hope would there be for your ever experiencing any lasting peace and happiness? My contention is that if a person will first play at the game of being an ideal individual in everything that is thought or done, then such a person will soon have more in the way of worldly goods than he really has any interest in. However, if he waits for the worldly goods to arrive before the greatness of character, he is almost sure to miss out on the goods and the greatness as well.

Currently any number of people feel they are being mistreated by life, and in one respect, at least, they are right. Many are suffering great personal discomfort and losing out on money each year. Sadly enough, however, these circumstances are often of one's own creating. For instance, there can be no happiness or progress while one nurses a grouch. Perhaps an unsatisfactory job is responsible for the grumbling. But can you imagine a grouchy disposition getting a person a better job? It has been my observation that the good jobs are rarely passed out to grumpy workers. A person should first get rid of grouchiness if progress is desired.

An observation made by Benjamin Franklin back in 1758 is appropriate to this line of thought:

> Friends ... Neighbours, the Taxes are indeed very heavy, and if those laid on by the Government were the only Ones we had to pay, we might more easily discharge them; but we have many others, and much more grievous to some of us. We are taxed twice as much by our *Idleness*, three times as much by our *Pride,* and four times as much by our *Folly,* and from these Taxes the Commissioners cannot ease or deliver us by allowing an abatement.

Here is an actual experience which ties in with this particular Franklin philosophy. A man I know of held an important position as an account executive with a prominent New York advertising agency. A well-educated, energetic and talented man, he was well paid for his services, and his promising future with his organization was taken for granted. He was one of the most dependable performers on the entire staff and was noted for being on the job early and late every day.

Suddenly a vacancy occurred near the top, and this man, along with many others, felt sure he would get this top-flight job. Apparently the management felt differently about the matter, because another member of the organization was appointed to fill the vacancy. This unexpected turn of events had a demoralizing effect on our account executive. He took it as a personal affront, and the injury to his pride was severe. When his cheerful disposition turned to surliness, his associates had an increasingly difficult time getting along with him. No longer the dependable member of the team, he began showing up late in the mornings, took more than his usual time for lunch and started leaving long before his regular quitting time.

The climax, however, was his taking an extra cocktail or two during his long lunch hours and several extra drinks on his way home. The drinks loosened up his tongue, which began to wag over the slight he figured he had received. His bitter criticism of the management for not appointing him to the coveted position was his real downfall. Word of his discontent spread around and, of course, filtered through to officers of the company. They put two and two together, decided they were paying big money to a dissatisfied staff member and concluded to discharge him.

Idleness, pride and folly reduced this man's taxes all right but at the hideous expense of liquidating his job. Shortly after getting him self fired, he would gladly have taken a position at one-half of his former salary. However, even a deal of this kind was not available, and the subject of my story spent many long, weary months in search of employment before finally taking a position paying about one-third of his previous income. His misfortune was surely of the self-inflicted variety.

Worry is another sure-fire producer of calamity. If money could be made with worry, there would be millionaires galore. But worry keeps at arm's length money and all the other desirable things of life. As someone has wisely said, "Worry is a don't-trust-God disease." Now I am not saying to readers, "Don't worry. Things could be worse." On the contrary, I am going to try to show that a far more scientific job of worrying can be done if a person will give some sensible thought to the matter.

I have long contended that people do not know how to worry properly. The country is full of frustrated part-time fretters who try to mix worry in with other things they are doing. For example, the businessman tries to sandwich worry into his work day. What's the result? Worry interferes with his business, and business interferes with his worry. As a consequence, he does not do a satisfactory job of either one.

The remedy seems to be very simple. The self-tormentor should set aside for himself a special time for worry. During this period he can stew and fret himself into a lather without interruption of any kind. Since one cannot make money with worry, quite naturally such a period should be established outside of business hours. This plan would enable an individual to carry on his business free from worry and also do his fretting entirely free from business interruptions. I invite you to try this experiment if worry is a problem with you.

Who Are You?

IN THE PRECEDING CHAPTERS I pointed out the feelings of tenseness, uncertainty and confusion that pervade the world today. I described my own success at getting rid of such impediments to happiness and indicated all along my belief that you can likewise be free of these disturbing emotions. Now let's turn our attention from me and concentrate on you. Let's find out what type of person you are.

Who are you? In answer to this question you would be able to relate quickly all vital statistics concerning your existence: your name, address, age, height, weight, birthplace, social security number, draft status, religion and educational background. But there is no need for me to bore you by enumerating the many things you could list. The point is that you could go on and on giving facts about yourself in an attempt to tell who you are.

However, if you account for all the facts relating to your existence, what would be the net result? It is true we could see whether you graduated from college, what neighbourhood you live in, how many children you have. But would this information give any better description of you than we could obtain by checking your credit rating card or looking at your personnel file? All this information can do is classify you and make you a statistic, so to speak, and I don't believe you would want anyone to judge you as a person solely on the basis of information to be found in a file. It is meaningless in telling just what kind of person you are. It would not reveal you as a loving father, a cheerful husband or a helpful friend.

There is much more to you than can be accounted for in statistics. Actually you are a rather complex structure: To the basic personality structure inherited at birth you have added an accumulation of memories of countless daily experiences that have taken place in your life, and since things are happening to you every day, you are constantly adding to your collection of memories.

After an event takes place in your life, it becomes a memory, which can be pleasant, painful or a matter of indifference according to the way you think about it. Thus, your thinking gives life to these memories; take away your thinking or your consciousness, and for you there would be no events and no memories of them.

Some people keep diaries and record in them the events that have taken place in their lives, generally with their reactions to these happenings. If you have ever read a journal, you know that you can get a comprehensive idea of the kind of person the diarist is because of what he has done and what he has thought about his experiences. Every person keeps a mental diary, whether he wants to or not, and each entry is a thought about particular experience. If the entries were written and one could read them, he would be able to tell these things about a person's emotional structure:

Vash Young

Likes and dislikes
Cheerfulness and gloom
Order and confusion
Tact and rudeness
Patience and irritability
Expectancy and hopelessness
Giving and getting
Exactitude and carelessness
Relaxation and tension
Harmony and discord

Daily entries in a diary for as long as you lived would make a rather lengthy history of your life. In the same manner, the collection of daily entries in your mental diary gives an extensive and complex story of your thought structure. Just as no one can duplicate the precise combination of events and impressions of another's diary, your thought structure is yours alone, for only you have had your particular collection of past experiences and your specific thoughts about each of them.

Statistical information is important in certain phases of your business and social life, but your thoughts are concerned in every aspect of your life. It goes with you on your business rounds each day, returns home with you at night, stays with you when you have your recreation on the golf course or at a party and even remains with you when you sit in church. Your own thinking is what you live with every day of your life.

Since thinking is the main ingredient in your make-up, it seems only reasonable that for you to do something about your life or personality you must start with your thinking.

We all know that boxers can condition their bodies in preparation for the physical test of a fight by training them to "take a punch" and by toughening them with a special diet. I believe you can condition your mind for the test of life by training it to take blows of disappointments and slights without flinching, and a diet appropriate to the mind is just as important to this type of conditioning as it is to the body. What better nourishment is offered for the development of a sturdy mind than the spiritual fare given to us by God, Who created us, gave us the capacity to think and in the Bible provided us with His thought-strengthening words?

The Future

MOST OF US seem to spend as much time thinking about what is going to happen as we do in reflecting on what has already taken place, for we are gravely concerned about the future and wonder what is in store for us. I believe it would be a much more constructive speculation, however, if we carefully considered what we hold for the future instead of what the future holds for us. If we have in mind a continuance of our past ways of life, are future results going to be satisfactory?

All you need do to answer this question is review carefully your present situation, and your will have just about the best answer obtainable. Everyone knows all about their past routines and the current results produced by them. If a person is satisfied with things as they are—satisfied that he has done and is still doing his level best—then he can continue with his past way of life and be assured of a fairly good future result. If, on the other hand, the individual knows within his heart he has not done his best in the past, it behoves him to change his ways for a better result later on.

Suppose that after careful self-analysis a man forty years of age concludes a change in his routine is necessary for him

to produce an improved situation in the years to come. Let's take a look at just a few of the difficulties involved, remembering that our subject has lived for forty years. He hasn't any soft job on his hands as revealed by the following statistics:

> *He has lived 14,610 days.*
> *Began forming habits the first day.*
> *Has been awake about 233,760 hours.*
> *Has entertained millions of thoughts and emotions.*
> *Has smoked perhaps 150,000 cigarettes.*
> *Has had maybe 36,000 drinks.*
> *Has eaten approximately 43,830 meals.*
> *Has been annoyed or upset perhaps 100,000 times.*

It is obvious that the fellow who wishes to make a change is going to need something beyond wishful thinking or mere will power to correct a routine established by day after day, hour after hour of habitual living similar to the foregoing outline. Suppose this man wants to go on a diet. According to the foregoing table, he has eaten approximately 43,830 meals. Interrupting an eating habit formed by this many trips to the table is a major undertaking. Is it any wonder then that a person is hardly fit to live with after a few days of dieting?

I know from experience that a person cannot get out of a rut simply by reading the newspapers, listening to the radio, watching TV shows, rushing off to business, engaging in round after round of social activities and doing a little wishful thinking about certain changes he would like to make in his way of doing things. He must be jolted out of a routine which does not contribute to his welfare.

In line with this reasoning, here is an idea I have presented many times from the lecture platform and also in one or two of my previous books. Let us assume you are notified that you have only one more day to live and your conduct on this final day would count in your favour or disfavour in the hereafter.

Under these conditions the millennium would promptly be introduced into your affairs. Like a devouring flame, it would destroy most of your handicapping thoughts, emotions and habits. Anxious to establish for yourself a favourable status in the hereafter, you would put forth a mighty effort to live an exemplary life for one day. Drinking, smoking, anger, resentment, faultfinding, chagrin, disappointment, frustration and everything else of a similar nature would be abandoned for this one last day. The moral is obvious. Simply look upon each day as your imaginary last day and conduct yourself accordingly. You can easily figure out for yourself the benefits of such a plan.

For one day, any person could overcome every handicapping thought or habit which has interfered with his happiness and success. What can be done once can be done again, and through daily practice we can bring about any change in our living routine necessary for a betterment of our current and future position in life. We all know very well that when death occurs, the body and all material possessions stay right here. In other words, we cannot take them along with us into the kingdom of heaven, assuming that is where we are headed. Therefore, we should actively concern ourselves with the one and only thing we can take with us, namely, our soul or character—call it what you will.

Like most people, I have given a great deal of thought to this situation, and one night not so long ago I decided to play dead. Without any trouble I disposed of myself as an individual. Except for my immediate family and a few close friends, I realized my death would not cause even a ripple anywhere and I would be quickly forgotten. I even likened myself to a grain of sand or a blade of grass, conceding that I wasn't any more important to the general scheme of things than either of these minutiae.

Next I contemplated my material body. There it lay absolutely complete in every way. The brain, heart, lungs, eyes, ears, nose, flesh, blood and bones were all intact but with no more ability to function than a car out of gas. I was reminded of this Biblical saying:

> As for man, his days are as grass: as a flower of the field, so he flourisheth. For the wind passeth over it, and it is gone; and the place thereof shall know it no more.

My corpse knew nothing about being the body of Vash Young. It did not know my family or friends, my business affairs, my many ups and downs. There were no regrets about the past and no concern over the future. Above all else, the body was something I could not take with me even if I wanted to. Having drawn this conclusion, I could continue with my fantasy. I imagined a doorkeeper stationed at the entrance to the kingdom of heaven. It was his duty to check the thinking of all those applying for admission. I wondered what chance I would have of getting in if my thoughts were characterized by fear, worry, selfishness, envy, jealousy, morbidness, self-torment, vain regrets, arrogance, sarcasm and greed. Not only did I conclude these worthless thoughts and emotions

Vash Young

would be denied admit but also I would not want to drag them around even if I could sneak them in.

I became convinced the gate to the kingdom of heaven would be thrown open to honesty, gratitude, cheerfulness, poise, tolerance, justice, humility, courage, love and all similar godlike qualities I was sure death could not affect. I reasoned that such a state of being not only would be welcomed into the kingdom of heaven but that it was available to us on this side of the grave at any time we wanted to let such qualities dwell within us. I saw very clearly that this state was something to live into and not die into.

The Ten Commandments

WE DO NOT have to guess about the type of thinking that is right for us because certain rules concerning our thoughts and thus our conduct have been given to us. The first rules that come to mind are the Ten Commandments. Since comparatively few individuals can recall them from memory, I am listing below six of them I wish to consider:

Thou shalt have no other gods before me.
Thou shalt not kill.
Thou shalt not commit adultery.
Thou shalt not steal.
Thou shalt not bear false witness against thy neighbour.
Thou shalt not covet thy neighbour's house nor any thing that is thy neighbour's.

Generally we follow these commandments, and obeying them is not too difficult for the majority of us. Let me explain what I mean. It is true that the first commandment is broken almost continuously by the common practice of catering first to the earth god called "Me". However, this mistake is not vicious, and with sincere practice we can put aside our selfishness and let God come first in everything we think and do. In regard to the second commandment, while murder cases regularly make the headlines, just think of the millions of people who do not kill. Though adultery is far more prevalent than it should be, again consider the millions who are not guilty of this sin. It is true the courts are kept busy dealing with those who steal, but how about the millions who conduct their daily affairs without stealing? While false witnesses do appear quite frequently in law suits, most of our citizens do not engage in anything of the kind. True, many people are perhaps envious of the possessions of a more successful neighbour, but countless millions are far too busy with their own problems to be at all concerned about a neighbour.

Therefore, I say again that as far as the Ten Commandments are concerned, most of us have nothing to worry about, but living in obedience to these commandments is by no means the answer to a peaceful, happy existence; it keeps us out of jail, and that is about all.

If we want to find out where we really stand, we should rate ourselves by what we do in relation to the Beatitudes. This beautiful pattern of life was given to us by the Saviour as part of His Sermon on the Mount:

Blessed *are* the poor in spirit: for theirs is the kingdom of heaven.

Blessed *are* they that mourn: for they shall be comforted.

Blessed *are* the meek: for they shall inherit the earth.

Blessed *are* they which do hunger and thirst after righteousness: for they shall be filled.

Blessed *are* the merciful: for they shall obtain mercy. Blessed *are* the pure in heart for they shall see God.

Blessed *are* the peacemakers: for they shall be called the children of God.

Blessed *are* they which are persecuted for righteousness' sake: for theirs is the kingdom of heaven.

Blessed *are* ye, when men shall revile you, and persecute *you*, and shall say all manner of evil against you falsely, for my sake. Rejoice, and be exceeding glad: for great is your reward in heaven: for so persecuted they the prophets which were before you.

Note the wonderful rewards involved in a conduct formula of this kind. The first one implies that those who are depressed by worldly prospects shall have the kingdom of heaven. This kingdom, the Saviour declared, "is within you". This conception could mean that a "kingdom of good things" may be ours here on earth, if we forsake the material for the spiritual side of existence. Instead of bewailing and complaining about our lot in life, we should arouse ourselves and thank God for our blessings. Then, we surely will be comforted.

It is said that the meek shall inherit the earth.

What a wonderful promise for those who go about their daily affairs free from anger, impatience, revenge, irritability and morbid sensitiveness! Meekness is true greatness, not servility. It is the ability to keep our passions and emotions under spiritual control. The inheritance of the meek is a way of life which transcends all material possessions.

It is promised that those who hunger and thirst after righteousness shall be filled. Just compare hungering and thirsting for right conduct to the usual practice of searching fretfully for material wealth, which rarely fills us with happiness and contentment. Righteousness is a form of nobility that keeps us on a straight course and assures a square deal to those with whom we have dealings, as well as to ourselves.

You will note that the way to obtain mercy is to be merciful. A merciful person is lenient, compassionate, kind, tender and helpful. The wonderful part of it is that these magnificent qualities are free, and they surely do enrich one's character.

The greatest reward of all goes to the pure in heart, since it is promised that they shall see God.

The word "pure" suggests these traits: cleanness, simplicity, innocence, modesty, genuineness, chastity, honesty. Filled with these majestic qualities, we can see God spiritually, for his invisible presence is surely made up of such virtues as these.

A great promise is made to the peacemakers, for they shall be called the children of God. The peacemaker is friendly, calm, quiet, tranquil, harmonious and amicable. What a satisfying experience would be ours if we went about our affairs with these qualities uppermost in our minds! We would truly be about the Father's business.

Persecution often follows those who turn to the right side of life for their happiness. For instance, the person who has stopped drinking may be ridiculed when sticking to soft drinks at cocktail parties. Also, keeping to the right in all business transactions may bring its share of unfriendly complications. However, the "persecuted for righteousness' sake" are to have the kingdom of heaven. To me this concept means that doing right brings the reward of having much inner peace in this earthly existence, regardless of the reactions of others.

Finally, you will note that great is the reward in heaven of those who, for the Saviour's sake, may be reviled, persecuted and spoken against falsely, "for so persecuted they the prophets which were before you."

Here in the United States we like games of all sorts, either as participants or as spectators. I would like to propose a game we can play right along with our daily chores — a game of genuine joy and lasting benefits.

I call it the game of "Secret Nobility":

Secret:-	Instead of:-
Bigness	*Smallness*
Courage	*Fear*
Strength	*Weakness*
Love	*Hate*
Cheerfulness	*Gloom*
Gratitude	*Grumbling*
Peace	*Discord*
Godliness	*Ungodliness*

By playing at this game all during our working hours, we will improve our relationships with others and at the same time automatically win the rewards that will comfort us. Keeping the Ten Commandments is a safe way of life; striving to live up to the Beatitudes is a stimulating way of life which brings blessings to others as well as to ourselves.

Exposing a Counterfeit

THE RIGHT THINKING and conduct called for by the Ten Commandments and the Beatitudes are the goals toward which we should strive, but impediments are placed in our way. We are unfortunately hindered by what I choose to call a "counterfeit".

At mention of the word "counterfeit", what is the first thought that comes to your mind? Probably you immediately think of spurious money, forgery, fake, a phoney and the like. Of the many definitions that could be given, I am going to pick out for my purpose the meaning "to carry on a deception".

In order to expose a case of counterfeiting, let us assume that you, a respectable, law-abiding, peace-loving citizen, are suddenly given the job of raising hell here on earth. Along with the job you are made invisible and given the power to influence the wills of human beings. You also have been endowed with all of the deceptive ingredients suggested by the word "counterfeit". Being the kind of person who does a job well, you take hold of this assignment of hell-raising among human beings with much gusto. As a measure of efficiency, you want to go about this work of yours without anything bothering you. You want a free hand and a clear field. Feeling that the Creator of the universe is likely to interfere with your plans, you will want to cut Him off from all the millions of people you have to work on. You decide that a good, thick smoke screen around the Almighty will do the trick, and with great energy you proceed with the job of enveloping the Supreme Being in a dense cloud.

You accomplish this deed by going among men, women and children of the world and planting in them the belief that their Creator is a vague, even imaginary character, located in a place called heaven, which also you label purely imaginary. You sell them on the idea that if He exists at all, He just sits up there far off and unavailable.

Having laid down this smoke screen, you set about separating Him still further from His children. Right here is where you put over one of your choicest bits of strategy. You find, of course, that many people are worshiping God or want to worship Him or have been taught that they should do so. This devotion is perfectly agreeable with you, because it gives you an added opportunity for hell-raising. You get busy right away, causing people to divide themselves into groups holding divergent religious opinions, creeds and beliefs. You then engender in each of these groups bigotry, intolerance, impatience and a disdain for the members of other religious groups. The resulting prejudice, contempt and persecution are very gratifying to you. You call to mind former days when stonings, burnings and all kinds of martyrdom took place. Having read in the Bible and in history books about such persecutions, you look forward gleefully to bringing about comparable conditions again.

In the meantime, you will find many incidents to amuse you, such as the girl who is denied a job because of her faith, frustrated marriage plans, friction in homes and sundering of nations over religious issues.

So far you are doing fine, working behind your smoke screen. However, you must get on with an extension of your program into other fields. Since doubt and bewilderment make a good foundation for trouble-raising, you now go ahead with more evil and general hellishness. You cause your victims to make sinful mistakes, for which they are punished. Thus, they will believe the Almighty is a harsh, unjust, unfeeling God; and for this mistaken reason, they will, of their own accord, withdraw further away from Him.

Having made them curse God because of the punishment for their own blunders, you bedevil them still further with another bit of artful deception. You cause them to feel remorseful and regretful over their mistakes, thus bringing them unhappiness through their self-condemnation and self-pity. There is nothing like vain regrets for getting a person down, and of course you know this very well. A sample of your handiwork would be the case of a young woman who, through ignorance and environment, makes a moral slip. She has not been able to hold her head up since her sin. She drags through the days considering herself an outcast. All she has to look forward to in her own mind is a lonely life of misery and regret. You would, of course, be particularly proud of this achievement.

With things going well all along the line, you now have another idea. Having effectively hidden from your victims their real God, you now get them to worship something more suitable to your ends. You come forth with a god guaranteed to work more havoc among your dupes than any other device you could possibly use. This god of yours is Money, which you make so alluring that you have no trouble at all in getting people all over the world to bow down and worship it. Its glitter and promise fascinate these worshipers. By dangling money before the eyes of earthly inhabitants, you accomplish more hell than by all the other things you have done put together.

You stand by and see homes broken up, friendships shattered, characters ruined. You see mortals resorting to all kinds of trickery in business deals; you see them stealing and even committing murder in their frenzied efforts to find peace and contentment in and through money. You see them feverishly building up money estates which are never big enough, never sufficient to satisfy them. You see them overindulge in the things money buys, only to find that these earthly treasures bring no lasting pleasures or happiness.

You have done some very effective work in making men, women and youngsters slaves to the getting habit. Their strained faces, their nervous habits, their tenseness and dissatisfaction all attest to the excellence of your efforts. Of course, you can deride your victims when they discover at the end of their days that despite all their struggles for riches, possessions, power and position, they cannot take one single item with them upon their departure from this earth.

Knowing full well that all things in both heaven and earth belong to the Creator, you would take fiendish delight in enticing men and women into the false position of attempting to take ownership into their own hands. You sell some of them on the idea of claiming a piece of the world for themselves, setting up their own ideologies and making a design of living for others to follow. You view with great pleasure the chaos caused by this bit of deception.

You are doing so well by now that it is easy for you to create discord in domestic relationships. At your bidding, businessmen heavily laden with the cares of the day go to their homes and give way to temperamental outbursts which, through necessity, they have kept in check during their business operations. The broken lives, broken hearts and family separations are very pleasing in your sight because this is all a part of your diabolical scheme.

It is a part of your plan to mislead God's children into believing they have been fooled in their devotions; their efforts to live up to His precepts have been in vain, with the promised reward nothing but a mirage.

Naturally, you would cause the inhabitants of the earth to make war one against the other with the inevitable ghastly results. Strikes, class hatreds, political and racial upheavals and other evils that might accompany war would be pleasing to you. Amid all this confusion, you could easily get millions of people to try to find relief from their troubles by turning to strong drink. You would line them up against bars and snare them into other drinking places. Then what a time you would have watching them expand, become bold and free, as the liquor gives a temporary boost to their morale! Later you would watch them degenerate as the liquor and their craving for it have devastating effects upon their bodies, minds and characters.

Having, by all these hellish machinations, dulled the senses of men to the true facts of life, having successfully kept them from establishing a protective relationship with their Creator, having completely hoodwinked them into an imaginary existence separate from the Almighty, having taken from them all hope of genuine happiness and freedom, you would have a gay time witnessing the complete havoc you have been able to achieve. You would have your mesmerized victims under complete control, blinded to all good, and you could pat yourself on the back over the realization that your job had been done well.

All that I have described and much more would happen if you were operating as an invisible hell raiser, instead of a respectable citizen. It is a filthy job you would not undertake under any circumstances, for you would not want to have anything so atrocious on your conscience. Neither would I, and neither would any other individual that we know of or can imagine.

What then do you make of such an ungodly mess? As you know, conditions like those I described actually exist today. It is axiomatic that there is no effect without a cause. Therefore, what is the sinister cause of this turmoil in which we are living? In my opinion, it is none other than the invisible counterfeit—Satan, devil, evil, or whatever name you care to give to the destructive influence which has been raising hell with human beings down through the centuries.

How the counterfeit of God ever got started I don't know. How it is going to be put completely out of business I don't know. But I do know the counterfeit sneaks off and leaves alone the individual who dares to stand up and fight it. Had I not proven this fact to my own satisfaction, I certainly would not be dealing with this worldwide issue. I don't expect my ideas on the subject to be of much use to the United Nations, for instance. However, I do hope my ideas will be of direct help to the readers of this book.

Here is a truth that I try to keep in mind constantly: Even though a counterfeit known as "Satan" is at work in the universe, God is functioning all the time. The thing to remember is that God is real, and the counterfeit unreal. If you do not watch closely, however, the counterfeit will seem to be more real and even more desirable than the Creator.

You can recognize the counterfeit because it is made up of selfishness, hate, arrogance, persecution, and lust for power, greed, bad temper, deceit, ignorance, destructive habits, worry, confusion, grief and boredom. Your history books give vivid accounts of the grief and turmoil caused by these evil tendencies working through generation after generation of people fooled into serving the fraud.

When you see a person who is angry, you see the counterfeit in operation under the name of the deluded individual. It will be well to consider just how you will make out by letting this deceptive nature govern your actions during your earthly existence. You can plainly see what has happened to the world and to millions of people who have been tricked into following the cheat.

True happiness can come only when you learn how to be like God in everything you think and do. However, the impostor has led many of God's children away from Him with fancy promises has caused them to forget God even exists.

With a few questions I want to suggest ways of fending off this counterfeit. For instance, you have been terribly unhappy. Why is it not possible for you to be correspondingly happy? You have been afraid. Why not be unafraid? You have been in despair. Why not be full of hope? Why ascribe more power to evil than to good? Why permit the kingdom of hell to be more real to you than the kingdom of heaven? Who makes your torment? Do you make it? Then why don't you stop making it?

The answer to these questions is that you are no more the creator of unhappiness than you are the creator of happiness. You are no more the creator of fear than you are the creator of courage. The choice between these opposite qualities is up to you, and you can be either like God or like the counterfeit.

In order that you may see what is necessary for you to be like God in the things you think and do, I invite you to look on Him in the following terms:

God is:

> *Love, Strength, Humility, Courtesy, Mercy, Justice, Joy, Freedom, Charity and more.*

How is this nature of the Creator going to be expressed on the earth unless God's earthly children exhibit these qualities in their daily affairs f You can either be like the Creator and receive the blessings He has in store for those who go about His business, or you can be like the counterfeit and receive the kind of pay this sham has been giving to human beings down through the ages.

The Greatest Wonder of All

I HAVE IMPLIED that to combat the counterfeit of God you should try to act more like God in your earthly affairs. Thus, if you are going to act like God, you would, in effect, be playing the role of His representative on earth. Have you ever given any thought to this idea of God's agent in the world? If you were asked to name that which represents God, what would you answer? Nature, churches, priests, rabbis, ministers? The answer is much more personal to you than any of these. You are God's representative on earth. This is the way the Creator made you, and you should accustom yourself to fulfilling this role. You should not shrink from this responsibility by saying that you are only a man, because the first chapter of Genesis tells you what you are as man in His likeness:

> And God said, Let us make man in our image, after our likeness: and let them have dominion over the fish of the sea, and over the fowl of the air, and over the cattle, and over all the earth, And over every creeping thing that creepeth upon the earth.

> So God created man in his *own* image, in the image of God created he him; male and female created he them.

It may annoy you even to have me call to your attention the foregoing Biblical quotations. You may feel inclined to say to yourself, "Who does this fellow think he is? He certainly has his nerve to direct my attention to something I have been

Vash Young

aware of most of my lifetime. I know what's in the first chapter of the Bible, perhaps even better than he does".

If this is your attitude, I would respond, "What have these two quotations done to you and for you? Have they changed the course of your life? Have they given you a sense of dominion over your business, domestic and social affairs? Have they made you feel you are a far greater marvel than any of the wonders on earth? Have they filled you with a daily glow, a gladness to be alive despite all the turmoil going on about you? Have they freed you from fear, worry and handicapping habits?" My contemplation of these verses has done all these things and much more for me.

Maybe it will help if you try to remember who is approaching you with this proposition. I am only a layman, a retired life insurance agent. I am the person who had to leave grammar school while in the fifth grade to start life as a fruit peddler. Currently I belong to no church, society or organization of any kind. I am neither a psychologist nor a psychiatrist. I have no medals and no degrees. I am not trying to promote anything. As a matter of fact, I am just a horse-and-buggy sort of person who has had an amazing experience with this proposition.

Like you, I have never seen God, nor have I heard His voice. Therefore, I can only go by what I think about these verses from the first chapter of Genesis. There you have the key to the fortune I have to share with you because my thinking about these two statements has turned hell into heaven for me right here on earth. It was my thinking about man in the likeness of God which saved me from committing suicide and enabled me to take a firm hold on the basic

98

proposition of *'How can I be more?'* instead of *'How can I have more?'*. That is, I decided to be more, in the image of God, rather than to have more, in the likeness of the counterfeit.

The daily application of this principle turned business failure into success for me. It gave me the confidence to face with calmness large lecture audiences without having a lesson in public speaking and to get five philosophic books out of my system with less than a fifth-grade education. My continuing belief in this principle enables me to feel like a youngster at the age of seventy. I concede that I may know little about the theological concept of God and man in His image and likeness. However, what I personally think about this greatest of all propositions gives me dominion over my current earthly affairs.

For the sake of making things easy for you, I wish I could say that the rather fantastic results I have experienced were brought about while I was reading a newspaper, listening to the radio, watching a TV show, gazing at a moving picture, chasing after business, sipping cocktails at some social function, thinking and talking about world conditions, or playing at some game. The fact is, however, that the change in my life and the results I have referred to did not come about in this way at all. At a time of great trouble, I ran smack into the two verses I have quoted from the Bible. This is what changed my life. I did not merely read these verses and go about my customary routine, waiting for things to happen. I applied this principle to everything I did and thought. I would still be aimlessly floundering about had I continued to devote all my time, energy and thought to the material routine I had been following for years.

I know what it is to experience most of the normal reactions to routine living, to blow hot and cold on things — being up one day and down the next. I know what it is to be the life of a party, to lead a barbershop quartet in boisterous song, with a few nice-tasting drinks oiling up the vocal chords. I was really very good at this. I know what it is to play poker, bridge, gin rummy, golf, and handball and sun myself at the beach. All of these things I have enjoyed as much as the next fellow. I have experienced the glow of putting over big business deals and receiving royalty checks. The thrills of seeing write-ups in leading newspapers and hearing the applause of lecture audiences ringing in my ears have been mine.

Though I have had my full share of excitement from the material side of life, I can say honestly that the most solid enjoyment ever to be mine has come about through my daily contemplation of God and man in His likeness. I openly acknowledge that I love God with all my heart, with all my soul and with my entire mind. This is not a deathbed confession to atone for a sinful life. It does not come at a time when I am old and worn out but rather when I am in the full bloom of my earthly career.

The Bible declares that "God is love". A state of being based on love, with its many meanings — affection, friendship, enthusiasm, fellow-feeling, sympathy, tenderness, liberality, charity and good will — became the kingdom of God to me. With this controlling idea in my mind, it was easy for me to experience the unspeakable joy of having such a kingdom within me right here on earth. How?

I was secretly:-	I became:-
weak	strong
sick	healthy
weary	refreshed
gloomy	cheerful
afraid	courageous
bored	vivacious
foolish	sensible
lazy	energetic
jittery	poised
envious	rejoiceful
trapped	free
a failure	a success

Simply by letting such thoughts and emotions dwell in my consciousness and govern my daily actions.

I boldly declare that any person who has within him the universally available kingdom of God I have within me can wipe out of his existence all the handicapping thoughts to which the human mind is subject. As one man's proof of this, please let me show you the amazing change which has taken place within me:

This new birth came about through my concept of man in the likeness of God. Atomic energy looms as a most powerful earthly force, but the spirit of God dwelling within one individual can blast out of his existence the counterfeit of God which has billions of victims all over the world.

Many people are patiently awaiting the return of Jesus in physical form. They seem to feel that with His presence a great many of our troubles would end. They did not end when He was here before, and all He got in return for His great mission was derision, ridicule, persecution, and finally He was nailed to the Cross. However, let us assume that Jesus does very suddenly make another earthly appearance. Just what effect do you think His appearance would have on the lives of people generally? Of course, if He began healing the sick, giving sight to the blind, causing the dumb to speak and the lame to walk, as He did before, great throngs would follow Him wherever He went. However, would the lives of men and women be made better if people only stood by and watched the Master perform again some of the miracles referred to in the Scriptures? Would people generally begin to love God with all their hearts and love their neighbour as themselves just because Jesus was back on earth? When He began to preach, what if He again used the Sermon on the Mount? Would His listeners immediately begin to follow that perfect design for living? Ask those questions of yourself. If your answers are negative, then you would not be benefited at all by the reappearance of the Saviour. The performance of His miracles before your very eyes would have no more effect on you than reading about them in the Bible.

When a child is kidnapped, a ransom is invariably demanded before the captive is released. Millions of men, women and children have been kidnapped and are being held as prisoners. Their prison bars are made up of stubbornness, self-will, sophistication, arrogance, pride, hate, envy, jealousy, revenge, fear, worry, discontent, unhappiness and a smouldering sense of injustice.

Living as Jesus lived to the best of our ability is the ransom God accepts for our release from this bondage. However, sitting complacently by, waiting for the physical return of Jesus, will never gain our release. If we accept the Sermon on the Mount as our pattern, adhering closely to it all through life, the Saviour will be brought nearer and nearer; soon His return will be actual to us, for we shall feel His presence within us and around us all through our days.

Is this a difficult proposition? Jesus said that His yoke was easy, and it is. Love surpasses hate as a means of getting along in life. Courage is far superior to fear. Purity is above sensuality. Meekness is much better than pride. Being merciful makes it possible to obtain mercy. Being a peacemaker makes life much easier than being a troublemaker. Right living produces far better results than wrong living. The proposition is that simple. The trouble is that we do too much praying and not enough acting like Christ. He has made everything simple and clear, and if we will but follow the plan he mapped out for us, our blessings will be many.

> But seek ye first the kingdom of God, and His righteousness; and all these things shall be added unto you.

Anyone who wants to can prove the truth of that statement. As far as I am concerned, the kingdom of God can be within us right in the midst of our earthly affairs, if we want it.

For instance, I know I am alive and have an awareness of things. I know my name, where I live and the amount of money that is in the bank to my credit. I know my family, relatives, friends and acquaintances. I know how to read the newspapers, watch TV, listen to the radio and go to the movies. All of this and much more is a part of my daily existence—something I am constantly aware of. At the same time, I am conscious of the existence of the kingdom of God right here on earth. As far as I am concerned, this state is just as real as my earthly existence. To me, love, courage, faith, hope, peace, unselfishness, justice, friendliness, purity and many other such qualities constitute the kingdom of God. I believe there is nothing at all mysterious about this kingdom dwelling within us here on earth. All we need do is open up our minds and let such a state exist within our consciousness.

Conclusion

I BEG YOU to consider deeply the ideas presented in the chapters "Exposing a Counterfeit" and "The Greatest Wonder of All". After revealing what I consider to be the invisible source of all trouble, I then tried to show how this universal troublemaker may be foiled. Judging from my own experience, I believe the ideas in these chapters are powerful enough to change the course of any life plagued with too much trouble. Even though you may not entirely agree with my thinking along these lines, I hope you will do some energetic thinking of your own about the real and counterfeit factors of existence. If life is not as you would like it to be, you certainly cannot bring about an improvement by merely sticking to your regular routine. The same old daily course of life must be changed if you are to get any real zest out of living.

As the majority of people follow their customary routines, something is strangely missing in their lives. For instance, on all sides we see the wonders of the universe, as referred to in the first chapter of Genesis, such as heaven, earth, sun, moon and animal life. These things are indeed wonders, but they are as commonplace to us as the nose on our face. We accept them as a matter of course and perhaps only occasionally view as wondrous a brilliant sunrise or a gorgeous full moon. But how about the greatest of all wonders, also referred to in the first chapter of Genesis: man made in the image of God and given dominion over the whole world? Do we see this wonder in our daily travels?

Of course, we see men and women rushing about in turbulent pursuit of their daily affairs. But do they express man in the likeness of God? It hardly seems so to me because, as a rule, these human beings do not exercise dominion even over their trifling personal affairs. Supply the answers to the following questions and prove to yourself whether these people are acting like man made in the image of God:

Is God:

> *Self-important?*
> *Disagreeable?*
> *Hard to get along with?*
> *Easily upset and annoyed?*
> *Envious and jealous?*
> *A slave to drinking and smoking?*
> *Sick and discouraged?*
> *Stubborn, opinionated, resentful?*
> *Secretly worried and afraid?*
> *Uneasy about the future?*

Of course, these phrases describe the attitudes of the majority of people you see going about their routine life, but we cannot think of the Creator in this way because such terms portray the nature and character of the counterfeit, the root of all trouble—personal, national and universal. What the world at large will ever do about this situation I do not know. But again I say that the individual can do something about it whenever the desire is strong enough for him to forsake the material for the spiritual side of life. Attention to the spiritual side of life is the answer to the many problems to which I have referred in previous chapters. For instance, take the chapter, "The Capital Value of Thought".

By looking on our thinking, instead of our bodily form, as the likeness of God, we can easily understand how our thinking is by far our greatest asset. Also, this concept enables us to keep out of our thoughts the emotional upsets which I pointed out were so destructive to certain individuals of my acquaintance.

In the chapter, "Sympathy for Business Leaders", I described the strain under which so many prominent men are labouring. Experience shows this strain is too much for the majority of our business and professional leaders. I believe their only salvation is to become humble and childlike and turn to the spiritual side of life for their support. I do not know of any other answer to the serious problems confronting most of our men and women in top-flight business positions.

I feel most people would follow the spiritual side of life if they only knew how. The trouble is that most grownups have only a Sunday school Conception of God and religion. This scant knowledge does not help them very much in times of trouble. They love God, go to church and are good citizens, but they do not understand man's relationship to God. What is more, they do not try to understand it; they leave this all-important issue for ministers to wrestle with. Moreover, people are so busy with their material affairs, the spiritual side of life becomes far removed from them.

What is to be done about it? That is the big question busy people would be justified in asking. That something should be done is quite obvious because, under this material routine, whole families run into trouble galore. Sickness, discontent, strain, fear, worry and even the breaking up of homes are just a few of the sad results produced when God is left out of our daily affairs.

Like most of you, I am only a layman, and I surely have been through the routine of life with a full share of ups and downs. But ever since my awakening I have been up, and I know I can stay up during the balance of my earthly existence. That which keeps me up is my concept of man made in the image of God. To me, this principle is no more complicated than the relationship of an earthly father and his son.

I believe there are many similarities between the father-son and God-man relationships. The earthly father loves his son and carefully guides him into correct ways of living. This is exactly what God does. Also, an obedient son looks up to his father and tries to imitate him in every way possible. By setting a proper example, a father has a good influence on his son and gradually moulds him into an upstanding citizen. If the son makes mistakes, does the father stop loving him? Not at all. Such a father forgives his son and patiently guides him out of the trouble he may be in. As a consequence, the son has increased love and respect for his father. A good father is never too busy to look after the welfare of his son, and a loving son is never too busy to show his appreciation in good deeds—not in idle words. This same type of relationship has been my experience with our kind and patient heavenly Father.

Thinking of one's self as man in the image of God is a powerful proposition. It certainly defeats that happiness-destroying counterfeit to which I have referred so many times. For instance, a hit-and-run driver recently rammed my parked car, leaving a big dent in it. I started to seethe over the incident until I got hold of my emotions with this line of reasoning: Was God angry about the situation? Of course, He was not. Then I immediately realized that the burning-up emotion was the counterfeit trying to slip into my consciousness. Also, I instantly concluded that the cost of repairing the damage was nothing compared to the loss in peace of mind I would suffer by getting into a mental lather over this matter. Having reached these conclusions, I had the car repaired and completely washed the experience out of my mind.

I have tried to act with similar emotional detachment in the management of my business affairs. Within recent years, I sold a home on Long Island we owned before coming to Florida. Also, I sold a home here in Florida, and this was my manner of handling these deals. After placing the properties on the market, I promptly assumed the attitude that God was the owner, the buyer and the seller. My position was simply that of caretaker. I determined not to forfeit my right to God's help by upsetting myself with impatience, concern about the real estate market, secret doubts and fears, or any other ungodly like thoughts and emotions. I held fast to this way of thinking, and the houses were quietly taken out of my hands and placed in the hands of a new caretaker.

The idea of my relationship with God also enabled me to conquer the drinking and smoking habits. I cannot imagine God so indulging Himself, and having a great desire to be as near like Him as possible, I can easily pass up these harmful habits. I find it much more fun proving my dominion over drinking and smoking than I ever had by yielding to these appetites. Not always have I been able to exercise such control, but I can certainly do it now. And I feel that anyone who wants to quit these habits can do so by holding fast to the idea of man as the likeness of God.

I could give numerous examples of the effective use I have made of this concept, which has indeed enabled me to forsake the material for the spiritual and thereby gain control over the temptations of life. The rewards of this type of life have been overwhelming for me, and I am sure they would be for anyone.

If all of us went after spiritual understanding as zealously as we seek material pleasures, the millennium would be introduced into our human affairs. For instance, people come down here to Florida intent on gratifying their desire for pleasure. They spend much time and money on three particular attractions: horse racing, dog racing and *jai-alai* games. There is nothing ungodly about these activities, nothing ungodly about watching them and, so far as I am concerned, and nothing too ungodly about gambling on the results of these sports.

To me, then, there is nothing wrong with these activities; they are simply forms of human diversion which are followed with great fervour. My observation has been that the results of these efforts for pleasure are unsatisfying. There is nothing of lasting value in them. The excitement of the racing finishes and the game is soon forgotten. But if the people who follow these sports spent as much time in pursuit of an understanding of their relationship to God, the reward would be a perpetual glow of happiness, absolutely unattainable in any other earthly activity.

110

Fortunes for All

To me one of the most vivid statements of how we can go about
our earthly affairs and at the same time maintain our proper
relationship to God is contained in Paul's magnificent
message as found in the thirteenth chapter of First
Corinthians :

> Though I speak with the tongues of men and of
> angels, and have not charity, I am become as
> sounding brass, or a tinkling cymbal.
>
> And though I have the gift of prophecy, and
> understand all mysteries, and all knowledge;
> and though I have all faith, so that I could
> remove mountains, and have not charity, I am
> nothing.
>
> And though I bestow all my goods to feed the
> poor, and though I give my body to be burned,
> and have not charity, it profiteth me nothing.
>
> Charity suffereth long, and is kind; charity
> envieth not; charity vaunteth not itself, is not
> puffed up,
>
> Doth not behave itself unseemly, seeketh not her
> own, is not easily provoked, thinketh no evil;
>
> Rejoiceth not in iniquity, but rejoiceth in the
> truth;
>
> Beareth all things, believeth all things, hopeth
> all things, endureth all things.
>
> And now abideth faith, hope, charity, these
> three; but the greatest of these is charity.

This quotation ties in perfectly with the idea of *'How can
we be more?'*, instead of *'How can we have more?'*. If we
are to *be* more, in God's image, rather than *have* more, in
imitation of the counterfeit, we cannot make a more

111

significant beginning than by applying the godlike virtue of charity in our daily existence.

I do hope that in this book I have aroused in you a new appreciation of yourself. Either you are man in the likeness of God, or you are not fulfilling the role for which you were created. Please reflect on this idea seriously and persistently, and you will become reborn. Best wishes to you for a new experience with life.